Disposable Heroes

Disposable Heroes

THE BETRAYAL OF AFRICAN-AMERICAN VETERANS

Benjamin Fleury-Steiner

ROWMAN & LITTLEFIELD PUBLISHERS, INC.
Lanham • Boulder • New York • Toronto • Plymouth, UK

Published by Rowman & Littlefield Publishers, Inc.
A wholly owned subsidiary of The Rowman & Littlefield Publishing Group, Inc.
4501 Forbes Boulevard, Suite 200, Lanham, Maryland 20706
www.rowman.com

10 Thornbury Road, Plymouth PL6 7PP, United Kingdom

British Library Cataloguing in Publication Information Available

Library of Congress Cataloging-in-Publication Data

Fleury-Steiner, Benjamin, 1970– .
Disposable heroes : the betrayal of African-American veterans / Benjamin Fleury-Steiner.
p. cm.
Includes bibliographical references and index.
ISBN 978-1-4422-1785-0 (cloth : alk. paper) — ISBN 978-1-4422-1787-4 (ebook)
1. African American veterans—Social conditions. 2. African American veterans—Services for. 3. African American veterans—Interviews. I. Title.
UB357.F64 2012
362.86089'96073—dc23
2012022921

™ The paper used in this publication meets the minimum requirements of American National Standard for Information Sciences Permanence of Paper for Printed Library Materials, ANSI/NISO Z39.48-1992.

Printed in the United States of America

Contents

Acknowledgments

None of the work presented here could have been possible without the participation of the veterans I was able to interview. I'm grateful for their generosity with their time and support of this book. Darryl Chambers, Yasser Payne, David Moseley (director of the Delaware Center for Homeless Veterans [DCHV]), and the National Association for Black Veterans (NABVETS) Baltimore, provided me with leads that resulted in numerous contacts with African-American veterans.

I want to thank my colleague Chrysanthi Leon, who from the project's earliest conception, helped me to organize my ideas and help recruit a cadre of talented undergraduates to assist in the transcription of early interviews. I also thank Joe Feagin, Michael Musheno, Jamie Longazel, Mona Lynch, Cal Morrill, Steve Herbert, Liz Brown, Ruth Thompson-Parker, and Forrest Stuart for thoughtful suggestions as this project developed. And my students Michael Akrong, Michael Burtis, and Anthony Gagnon for their combined efforts in transcribing numerous interviews over the better part of two years.

My editor Sarah Stanton deserves special thanks for her strong support of this project from its earliest stages.

Kristen Hefner did an excellent job completing the index and provided invaluable feedback in the final stages of preparing the manuscript.

I thank my parents, Phyllis and Howard Steiner, for their unconditional love and support throughout my pre- and post-military years. And to my loving spouse, Dr. Ruth Fleury-Steiner, and our wonderful daughters, Anna and Robin: words cannot express how lucky I am to have you in my life.

Chapter One

African-American Veterans and the War at Home

Jackson:	My mother got very sick and eventually passed away in like '96. That changed everything. I was going to a community college using the GI Bill and had to drop out and move back to New York City. And you think it's bad here? Well this place is Disney Land compared to the Bronx [laughs]! Anyway, my mom left me the house but she still owed $48,000 on it. So, I started renting it out—I mean, I could use the money—but the people started messing up, smoking crack, and weren't paying the rent, so I lost the house and that's when it began—when I was first homeless.
Joe:	There's bills to pay, people living around here are still the same—unemployed, drinking and drugging, mostly—and my mom's been real sick. She's in the hospital and doing better now. But pretty soon you know you just sit around all day, and become a part of the furniture and what have you [laughs].

"I LOST THE HOUSE AND THAT'S WHEN IT BEGAN"

At the time of our interview, Jackson[1] (age 42) had been living at Independence House (IH) for nine months. He greeted me in a gray U.S. Army physical training (PT) sweat suit. As a former enlisted U.S Army Reservist in the 1990s, PT sweats were a "second uniform" to me and many others who served.

Interviewer: I see you still got your PT gear. I miss wearing those!"

Jackson: Oh yeah, you served?"

Interviewer: Yep, army, 95 Bravo, military police. In the early 1990s, I served in the reserves and did a short stint in Saudi Arabia during Operation Desert Storm.

Jackson: So, you were in the desert too?! I was over there watching the fireworks. But you don't look like the service type, Mr. Professor [laughs].

Interviewer: Yeah, it was another life . . . But thank goodness for those Patriot missiles! Those scud attacks were crazy. But you're right there were some serious fireworks to watch over there.

There was nothing especially unique in this exchange with Jackson. In fact, it was the kind of ice breaker that I've had many times with other army vets I've met over the years; one that invariably begins with a firm handshake and a brief talk about one's branch of the service and military specialty. Instead, two things surprised me about Jackson. First, was his appearance: he seemed to be favoring his right leg throughout our interview and his numerous missing teeth made me think he had to be at least ten to fifteen years my senior or more, instead of only three years older (I was 39 at the time of our interview). What caught me off guard the most was revealed in our next exchange:

Jackson: You still in?

Interviewer: No I got out in the late 90s.

Jackson: I'm supposed to be at drill next weekend. But I'm dealing with a lot health issues lately. My legs been swelling up and the dental stuff [opens mouth] is from my diabetes. So I may be heading to the VA hospital. . . . But I'm a lifer and would love to go active duty again if I could. In fact, I wish I could go to Iraq. I mean, when I'm ready to.

Why my surprise at Jackson's continued service in the reserves? For one, he lives at IH, a sober temporary housing facility in an extremely impoverished section of Wilmington, Delaware, whose residents are all male and virtually all African American. It is here in IH's computer room where Jackson and I first met.

Interviewer: How did you wind up here?

Jackson: My mother got very sick and eventually passed away in like '96. That changed everything. I was going to a community college using the GI Bill and had to drop out and move back to New York City. And you think it's bad here? Well this place is Disney Land compared to the Bronx [laughs]! Anyway, my mom left me the house but she still owed $48,000 on it. So, I started renting it out—I mean, I could use the money—but the people started messing up, smoking crack, and weren't paying the rent, so I lost the house and that's when it began—when I was first homeless.

Interviewer: Did you have any relatives or friends who could help you out?

Jackson: No, my dad died when I was sixteen, and I haven't seen my sister in eight years. So, that's it. I'm on my own and have to survive. I am a survivor. But with this I got in over my head with the house, but I was not around to make sure things were kept up. And before I knew it was taken from me.

Interviewer: Was it because reserve duty created too many obligations?

Jackson: That and I started to suffer from depression and PTSD, which I think only got worse after mom died. I started drinking a lot more than I usually do, which obviously didn't help. Plus, I learned that I'm not a very good slumlord [laughs].

Interviewer: What about the VA [U.S. Veteran's Administration]?

Jackson: Well, yeah, I see them for counseling and get some meds for depression and have stayed in the VA hospital, but that's only temporary. But I don't receive any [benefits] because my PTSD isn't combat related.

Interviewer: So take me back to after you lost the house.

Jackson: I lived in a van that I still had. And then I would have reserve duty and I got a job doing some painting on a military base in upstate. So it was not a set schedule, and I started taking the bus to cut down on gas money. This neighbor let me store the van in their back yard. But the police ended up taking it, because they said the vehicle had to be up on cement.

Interviewer: So no more van. . . . Oh, man.

Jackson: Yeah, so I had nothing left up there but I knew some people in Delaware. So I ended up getting some bus fare together to come down here. Living with those friends didn't work out because they wanted to start charging me rent. So, I stayed in a breakfast mission. And then I started doing different jobs with a temporary agency like working in a warehouse and for an electric company. But I was making too much money and wore out my welcome there, so they kicked me out. And that's when I started sleeping on the riverfront. There was a big concrete block down there right by the bridge that was my house [laughs]. But I had a hernia and I had to get an operation at the VA hospital. And when I got out it was winter. I mean, I had an army tent so I could survive anything down there, but it was cold! Fortunately, I was able to get a bed here, otherwise I'd still be down there living by the river.

Interviewer: Wow. . . . So I've got ask you, just driving around here seeing so many black people living either under the bridges or packed together in substandard housing, how does that make you feel as a black veteran?

Jackson: It's crazy, man. I joined up to get out of here and make something of myself, but things didn't work out. . . . I gotta keep pushing on, but being here is real hard. . . . But this place and poor, black vets? That ain't even on people's radar. You know it's like when we go out on bivouac [overnight military exercises conducted in typically remote areas] no one knows where the hell you are. It's like that out here, only people are starving and suffering for real, you know what I'm saying?

Interviewer: Yeah. . . . How are you doing health wise?

Jackson: My feet are swollen up pretty bad and my dental is messed [lifts up lip to show missing teeth]. . . . Hopefully, I'll get over to the VA tomorrow.

Interviewer: Okay, but I'm going to inform the director on my way out.

Jackson: He knows my deal. I'll be alright.

The next week after I returned to IH, I followed up on Jackson's condition. Sure enough it was long-term complications from diabetes, hypertension, and excruciating chest pains. Fortunately, Jackson had been transferred to Perry Point VA Medical Center (Maryland) for longer-term care. On the other hand, from a sociological perspective his story was compelling on many levels. Jackson's words give life to broader conditions characterized by profound racial inequities in housing, heath, and indeed, wealth. Although Jackson was transferred to a well-respected VA hospital for long-term care, this young man of 42 years had obviously been suffering *needlessly* for years. He may have "special benefits" that provide him access to emergency health care, but Jackson describes his situation as "real hard" and the broader conditions as one of extreme isolation where "people are starving and suffering for real." Jackson suffers from individual trauma (e.g., Post Traumatic Stress Disorder [PTSD]),[2] serious health problems such as untreated diabetes, and the lasting pains of collective traumatic experiences, such as having to live in a racially aggrieved neighborhood. His story also shows, as we'll see in the lives of numerous other veterans of color, experiencing the loss of a loved one as a subsequent plunge into downward mobility or homelessness.

Yet Jackson is confident that he will "be alright." Rather than simply defining stories of "victims" or "deviants," African-American veterans are survivors even in the face of dire life circumstances. Consider the story of Joe, another a veteran of color who lives with eight family members in an overcrowded Section 8 housing development in another marginalized section of the city. Joe (age 36) is a veteran of the first Gulf War and recently completed nearly two years of service in Iraq. Since returning to the United States, Joe struggles with PTSD and chronic unemployment, but in the months just prior to our interview he began working as a part-time mechanic and is using his GI Bill benefits to take classes at a local community college.

"IT'S SO FAR, SO GOOD"

Interviewer:	So how were you able to turn it around?
Joe:	I finally got my ass to the VA. They were real helpful.
Interviewer:	But why did it take nearly two years?
Joe:	It was different this time. I mean, I never much cared for the whole VA bullshit, but when I got home from Iraq things were different; I actually saw many people over there. But I still wanted to put all that behind me and just pick up where my life left off. But it ain't that easy. There's bills to pay, people living around here are still the same—unemployed, drinking and drugging, mostly—and my mom's been real sick. She's in the hospital and doing better now. But pretty soon you know you just sit around all day, and become a part of the furniture and what have you [laughs].
Interviewer:	How did the VA help to get you off the couch then?
Joe:	I just stayed persistent with them. And my counselor was cool. She helped me get on a schedule with therapy and I learned about all these benefits I have. I don't have a car yet, definitely on the lookout for one now, but I figured out the bus route to get to classes and the GI Bill's taking care of

> that. So, you know, I'm starting to get on track. . . . I was a mechanic in the military and working part-time in a garage now, but I'm hoping with these business classes that I'll learn the best way to start my own business and open my own shop one day. But back to what you were asking, it's good to have some support from the vet center. . . .
>
> It's so far, so good.

Disposable Heroes begins with a simple observation: For a grossly disproportionate number of African-American soldiers, the end of military service signals a return to a largely unforgiving civilian world that has little use for them. This observation takes on a special significance when one considers the experience of black veterans who enlisted in the military to escape the ravages of racial segregation and social immobility. At the heart of *Disposable Heroes* are interviews with thirty African-American men who served in the military from the Vietnam and All Volunteer Force (AVF) eras. This rich life history data is at the heart of the book. Although I have intentionally avoided discussing my own experiences as veteran, I would be remiss if I didn't at least briefly describe the time when I returned home from the service. As a veteran of Operation Desert Storm who is nearly the exact same age as Jackson, I believe a brief overview of my own journey home provides an important contrast. As the opening dialogues reveal, the entire experience of researching and writing this book has been, in a word, edifying. I was simply ignorant of the extent to which racial marginality continues to be perpetuated in the African-American community in general and in the lives of black veterans in particular.

In considering my own experience as a white veteran in the early 1990s who returned to a middle-class suburban community, I was able to bounce back quickly. Ultimately, I can conclude that the military had enormously positive implications for my own post-service life experiences. While I did harbor feelings of mistrust toward the military, especially the VA, my transition to civilian life was far smoother. Considering Jackson, who is still in the service, when I finished my commitment I had no desire to reenlist. My subsequent use of the GI Bill, moreover, allowed me to be resilient in a way that I just assumed was characteristic of most, if not all, veterans. Although, things are "so far, so good" for impoverished African-American veterans like Joe, the stakes of failure for me were obviously far less than for Joe. Furthermore, Joe must confront the personal anguish and uncertainty of having his only parental figure in the hospital (although, he didn't show any, I know it would be extraordinarily difficult on me).

My more than two-decade journey from undergraduate to doctoral student to sociology professor had everything to do with my ability to exploit my own middle class, white privilege. For one, when I first returned home I could *take time off* from the world of education and work and live *rent free* in my parent's house without the slightest pressure from my loving and supportive family and friends. The benefits of being the white son of parents from middle class suburbia had everything to do with understanding how I was able to rebound so quickly. In contrast to both Jackson and Joe, as an unemployed 21-year-old veteran I was able to avoid the VA and use my parent's far more flexible private health care plan. While I had always struggled with anxiety, and to be sure, it clearly became more of a challenge after returning from the Persian Gulf in the spring of 1991, I had access to excellent mental health care and was able to take the time to rest in the absence of the kinds of awesome pressures experienced by both Jackson and Joe.

In fact, within only a few months I found myself, as many privileged white twenty-somethings, longing to leave the "womb." So when I say "privileged," I mean unequivocally that *I didn't have to worry about anything*—once my GI Bill papers were in order, everything else took care of itself. And *even if things didn't work out*, my parents had paid off their house, so I could always stay there rent free and take more time to reassess my life. So leaving the suburbs and returning to college in the summer of 1991—indeed, only a few months after coming home from Operation Desert Storm—seemed perfectly *natural* to me. The experiences of young, marginalized African-American veterans such as Jackson, Joe, and numerous others illuminate how race deeply matters. But more than stories of helpless victims, Joe and Jackson see their glasses as half-full. At the same time, both men's lives are characterized by a series of *interconnected traumatic experiences* (e.g., profound housing inequalities, loss of a loved one, and other health-related crises). What they have experienced—perhaps, especially Jackson, although Joe lives in profoundly substandard housing conditions—in their post-military lives is far closer to what sociologist Kai Erikson famously characterized as individual *and* collective trauma:

> By individual trauma I mean a blow to the psyche that breaks through one's defenses so suddenly and with such brutal force that one cannot react to it effectively. . . . The collective trauma works its way slowly and even insidiously into the awareness of those who suffer from it, so it does not have the quality of suddenness normally associated with "trauma." But it is a form of shock all the same, a gradual realization that the community no longer exists as an effective source of support and that an important part of the self has disappeared.[3]

While Erikson's conception was formulated in the devastating wake of a singular traumatic episode (e.g., the Buffalo Creek Flood), it is clear from his seminal research that trauma works as a profoundly social process. Well beyond individual exposure, trauma eats away at community efficacy in the lives of residents. Erikson's story is, however, also not one of one-dimensionally "helpless victims." Community members' resilience and agency are on full display, especially the role of religious faith in their post-disaster lives. The challenges of collective efficacy in marginalized communities of color is well documented in the sociological literature,[4] however, a more dynamic conception of the lives of members of marginalized communities are, with some notable exceptions,[5] given far less attention. This is all the more surprising when one considers that members of marginalized communities of color live complex lives, for example, as job seekers.[6] A lack of attention to challenging post-military experiences is especially problematic in the case of marginalized veterans of color, many who have endured the pains of racial inequality for decades (e.g., Vietnam era veterans).

THE BETRAYAL OF AFRICAN-AMERICAN VETERANS

Since the Vietnam era, black veterans continue to be denied basic benefits and are subjected to a myriad of racial inequalities, including vastly unequal employment opportunities, health care inequity, and being forced to live in grossly substandard housing conditions.[7] In a word, for generations the actions of white wartime political elites have been devastating. Consider the brutal campaign in Vietnam. Despite the growing body counts, General William C. Westmoreland routinely appeared in the media stating falsehoods about the "steady progress" the U.S. military was making in Vietnam. As late as November of 1967, President Johnson's U.S. ambassador to South Vietnam, Ellsworth Bunker, expressed optimism in the prospects for U.S. "victory."[8] In the case of African-American Vietnam era veterans, the Johnson administration's Project 100,000—a strategy conceived by the controversial Democratic senator and sociologist, Patrick Moynihan—focused on the aggressive conscription of poor, unskilled urban blacks. Such a sweeping racialized approach to governing impoverished blacks through the draft was by all accounts a devastating failure:

> Project 100,000 turned out to be one of the most shameful aspects of our Vietnam policy. Seldom mentioned was the fact that a disproportionate number of Project 100,000 men entered combat. Their combat force helped stave off the politically nettlesome possibility of dropping student deferments or calling up the reserves. The much touted training skills were seldom taught. The program sent several hundred thousand to Vietnam and several thousand to their deaths. The most volatile aspect of the program was *race* [emphasis added]. . . . A 1970 Defense Department study disclosed that 41 percent of Project 100,000 men were black, compared with 12 percent in the armed forces as a whole. . . . After the war, Project 100,000 men who survived slipped back into the world of the subterranean poor.[9]

President Richard Nixon did little to assist the lives of impoverished Vietnam veterans of color. Indeed, Nixon let the brutal war rage on into the early 70s and simultaneously defunded veteran centers and treatment facilities. Moreover, the inaugural "war on drugs" sowed the seeds of the mass incarceration of blacks in the decades to come. President Ronald Reagan's betrayal began with an unprecedented ramping up of the drug war and simultaneous cuts to veteran benefits. Only a few years into his first term in the early 1980s, Reagan's budget director, David Stockman, "with one stroke of his pen . . . wiped out the entire readjustment counseling program, in effect thumbing his nose at 39,000 veterans who had already obtained help, as well as the million more (by some estimates) who needed it."[10]

Despite vocal opposition by some of the nation's most decorated veterans, President George H. W. Bush launched the first Gulf War, Operation Desert Storm. One of the most disturbing legacies of this era is that tens of thousands of veterans continue to suffer from debilitating symptoms of "Gulf War sickness." Not surprisingly, Bush continued to escalate the drug war with hysterical references to a "black crack epidemic" and redoubled Reagan era fiscal policies that barely kept racially aggrieved communities above water. President Clinton's administration escalated the war at home and simultaneously denied tens of thousands of Gulf War veterans health benefits. After taking control of the House, Speaker Newt Gingrich declared any financial support to the families of Vietnam veterans as "wasteful spending." Moreover, while Clinton's presidency is typically associated with greater employment opportunities for African Americans, recent research demonstrates convincingly otherwise: "Only by counting the penal population do we see that fully two out of three young black male dropouts were not working at the height of the 1990s economic expansion."[11] Numerous volumes have provided important and scathing critiques of George W. Bush's prosecution of the war in Iraq.[12] However, few have connected this senseless conflagration to domestic policy at home. One exception is Frances Fox Piven's remarkable book, *The War at Home: The Domestic Costs of Bush's Militarism.* Considering the current economic meltdown and unprecedented wartime spending, Fox Piven's argument remains especially prescient today:

> Explanations focusing on imperialism assume the main reason for war in Iraq was to shore up American domination abroad. I argue that another reason for war was to shore up America's rulers at home. . . . [W]ith the political lift gained by war-making, the Bush regime was also able to push rapidly ahead with its right wing domestic policy agenda [of] extracting wealth from the American people.[13]

The extraordinarily costly wars in Iraq and Afghanistan have had devastating human and economic consequences for the home front. This is especially so for those who have toiled in poverty on the margins of society for decades.

The stories of older African-American veterans from the Vietnam era, as I will present in subsequent chapters, brings into sharp focus the deepening racial inequalities of the contemporary post-Bush civilian world. Wallace Terry's enduring observation of nearly three decades ago continues to resonate in the second decade of the twentieth century: "[W]hat can be said about the dysfunction of Vietnam on veterans in general can be doubled in its impact upon most blacks; they hoped to come home to more than they had before; they came home to less."[14]

The stories of African-American veterans take on a special urgency in this current era of spiraling economic inequalities and seemingly endless wars. Like their counterparts from Vietnam, the latest generation of black veterans also *returns home to less*. Indeed, in the years since the conflagration in Vietnam, African-American incarceration rates, unemployment, and poverty have dramatically increased.[15] Veterans return to socioeconomic conditions today that are, in a word, profoundly distressing. Although African Americans make up roughly 12 percent of the U.S. population, Department of Defense statistics reveal that disproportionate numbers have been killed or seriously wounded in Iraq and Afghanistan.[16] During this same time period, African Americans lost an astonishing half of their total net worth, and while overall unemployment rates have increased for all Americans, jobless rates among blacks are double those of whites.[17] According to a recent Department of Labor report, African-American veterans are grossly overrepresented among the unemployed.[18] Despite the election of the first African-American president, there is no coordinated policy to address the explosive conditions of what can accurately be called the *New Jim Crow*.[19]

OBJECTIVES OF THE BOOK

The book's primary objective is to focus on the post-war experiences of black veterans as told in their own words. In particular, I provide rich life histories of African-American veterans' pre- and post-military experiences. Specifically, these detailed dialogues illuminate historically contextualized situations and conditions that are far more than a collection of individual "war stories." When viewed together, *Disposable Heroes* presents an indictment of a longstanding legacy of dehumanizing social conditions that African Americans have endured for generations. And in the case of black veterans, the combined pains of readjustment into civilian society means continued racial oppression; for Vietnam era veterans it means experiences with overt Jim Crow racial segregation and in the case of AVF era veterans the "New Jim Crow" of white backlash toward integration and mass incarceration.

At the same time, many *African Americans have benefitted remarkably from their service in the military*. Their service has resulted in unprecedented social mobility. Yet as the stories in this book make clear, black veterans are needlessly forced to endure a number of racialized deficits. They have endured white racial oppression and subsequent forced ghettoization, a sweeping backlash against racial integration efforts, and the devastating wars on drugs and crime.

HOW THE CURRENT PROJECT EVOLVED

This project began in the fall of 2009 at IH, an all male, temporary housing facility located on the fringe of one of the more impoverished and racially isolated sections of the city of Wilmington, Delaware. I learned about African-American veterans living there at a meeting arranged by a colleague who subsequently arranged a meeting with me; my colleague Dr. Santhi Leon, IH's (now former) executive director; and a local representative from the Wilmington VA. I learned at the meeting that many black veterans had recently moved into IH as part of the VA's emergency beds program. My initial interviews were arranged by IH's executive director. Before providing more background detail, it is important to describe IH and the surrounding neighborhood.

To the uninitiated, getting to IH is quite an adventure. For one thing, the street where the facility is located requires special access to enter through the police-monitored gate. Most non-residents, including myself, must continue past IH and loop around down the next street. After passing a stretch of three or four boarded up, abandoned houses, a sign of heading in the right direction appears. Signs of inferior housing abound. The neighborhood is filled with small, tightly clustered rows of older housing tenements with broken or dangling front door frames, cracked windows, and black soot that has stained gray their chipped, white paint exteriors. And much like the conditions of social isolation described by generations of African-American sociologists who wrote about such racially aggrieved neighborhoods in cities throughout the United States[20], there are typically very few people present on the street. Indeed, just as in these classic accounts, when residents do appear they typically are in groups of young black men congregated on street corners.

A feeling of hopelessness in the neighborhood was palpable, especially from the perspective of a privileged white person who has spent little time in this section of the city. Wilmington is a tiny city, so IH's entryway sign was easy to spot, even from the next block. But what makes this converted old housing project conspicuous is its large grassy lot. Measuring about half the size of a football field, IH's front yard stands out on a street that is otherwise entirely concrete. Tucked in one corner are a few picnic tables for residents to smoke cigarettes or play cards. And lining the chain link fence at the back of the property is a collection of duffel bags and black plastic garbage bags; many of the latter hang from IH's chain link fence. What I thought was trash, was actually overflow storage for several residents. As the facility's director explained to me, "We just don't have adequate storage room in this building, so it's up to those men to find space for that stuff. It's an eyesore out there. But I've already warned them that it is going to be tossed if it isn't removed soon." The bags did remain for a few more weeks, but true to the director's word the fence was spotless by the next week. Just inside the door sit a large security desk with three video monitors, shelves stuffed with bus schedules, and a bulletin board with employment postings (e.g., typically warehouse work at various chain wholesale stores). In addition to a narrow bench where men sometimes sit and talk, the first floor hallway has three bedrooms that have been converted into staff offices and a closet turned into a makeshift computer room.

EXPANDING THE SAMPLE BEYOND RESIDENTS OF INDEPENDENCE HOUSE

After completing multiple life history interviews at Independence House (IH) with African-American veterans, I broadened my inquiry to the city's other mostly impoverished, nearly all black neighborhoods. An early lead came from Delbert, a 65-year-old Vietnam era veteran, whom I interviewed at IH. Delbert put me in touch with veterans at the Wilmington VA. The next interviews were thus completed via snowball sampling that began with informal meetings in the Wilmington VA reception area, a location that Delbert had informed me was a popular hangout for black veterans waiting to attend various classes or therapy sessions. I arranged for several interviews with black veterans from both the Vietnam and AVF eras which, in turn, created additional leads. By early 2010, I struggled to find more African-American veterans who were willing to be interviewed. However, this drought ended after a colleague put me in touch with a Cold War era veteran, Gerald, who, in turn, connected me with Vietnam era veteran Mel. Next, I decided to go outside Delaware and put an inquiry in to the Baltimore Chapter of the National Association of Black Veterans (NABVETS) which subsequently was answered (unfortunately, Delaware does not currently have a NABVETS chapter). My interview with Baltimore-based veteran, Lionel, was conducted over the course of two telephone conversations. The final interviews were conducted by telephone with African-American veterans of Operation Iraqi Freedom.

A CLOSER LOOK AT THE SETTING

It is critical to understand in more detail the housing conditions and surrounding areas in which I conducted the bulk of the in-person interviews with African-American veterans. Wilmington, Delaware, is a city with a volatile racial history. The race riots of 1968 burned sizable portions of the city to the ground. From April 5, 1968, to January 21, 1969, 3,500 National Guard troops occupied Wilmington.[21] Today, the city remains characterized by extreme levels of racial segregation and concentrated poverty.[22] With a population of approximately 70,000 residents, it is one of the only metropolitan areas in the nation in the last twenty years to add *an additional high poverty census tract*. Despite the presence today of some new mixed-income developments, a very high number of decaying tenements and large stretches of long-abandoned industrial sites overshadow these efforts at redevelopment.

The stubborn prevalence of concentrated poverty and racially isolated neighborhoods in the "City of Skyscrapers"—a nickname given to Wilmington for its numerous bank and credit card industry buildings that fill its skyline—began in the wake of the devastating civil rights riots of 1968 and have grown ever since.[23] Most recently, Mayor James Baker Jr., a former civil rights activist and lifelong resident of the city, and the Wilmington Housing Authority (WHA) have aggressively used federal funds obtained through the U.S. Department of Housing and Urban Development's (HUD) Housing Opportunities for People Everywhere (HOPE VI) program[24] to demolish substandard public housing units in the sections of the city's lower income neighborhoods. Although Mayor Baker and the WHA's efforts at urban renewal have resulted in dramatically improved housing for some residents of these neighborhoods, popular pressures to aggressively crack down on drug and gun-related violence have been prioritized over housing, especially in the city's poorest neighborhoods.[25]

According to the *City of Wilmington's Five-Year Strategic Plan (FYSP) 2011–2015*,[26] 2,282 applicants remain on the public housing waiting list, a full 98 percent of whom are very low income, and 87 percent of applicants are African American. Instead of creating more housing for this population, city officials have concentrated on housing-related services (e.g., temporary housing), although there is no substantive plan for such expansion outlined in the *FYSP*. Instead, the report calls for "greater law enforcement and efforts to respond to the social, economical, educational, and personal responsibility factors that contribute to the drug trade and gun violence."[27]

PLAN OF THE BOOK

Chapter 2, The African-American Veteran as a Social Problem, sets the stage for the rest of the book by providing both relevant historical background and a few glimpses into the present-day lives of African-American veterans. By highlighting complex agency in the lives of respondents from different generations, the objective is to show the difficulty inherent in discussing "people as problems." Most important, the goal of the chapter is to introduce black veterans of the Vietnam and Iraq wars to highlight the need for a more expansive, life history-centered inquiry.

Chapters 3 through 5 are organized to present both the experiences of African-American Vietnam and AVF era veterans. By "all AVF era," I refer to a dramatic change in military service from 1973 to the present. Specifically, after the Vietnam War had ended, the U.S. military changed from conscription to voluntary recruitment of soldiers. While I try to stay focused on a thick presentation of this data as it unfolded during the course of the interviews I conducted, some of the veterans I interviewed were less forthcoming. In this instance, I either use particular parts of their interviews to accent more detailed material presented or to omit what I've determined to be overly vague or redundant responses. To provide continuity across each of the data-centered chapters, I try to present material from the most complete interviews conducted (e.g., veterans who provided the richest information on their pre- and post-military experiences).

Chapter 3, Joining Up, presents veteran's stories of their formative years with particular attention to the events that led to their decision to join the military. In the case of Vietnam era veterans, some respondents were conscripted, so they did not choose to enlist in the military. However, both conscripted Vietnam era veterans and those who enlisted on their own provide important insights into conditions of Jim Crow segregation at a time of war and radical social instability in the United States. AVF era veterans provide a fascinating array of stories that link experiences with broader historical conditions of racial marginality with often unexpected entryways into the service. Other AVF veterans describe the decision to enlist in far more positive terms, such as achieving a major goal they had set for themselves during high school.

Chapter 4, In the Service, focuses on African-American veterans' experiences in the military. Here, veterans tell visceral tales of life in and out of a combat theater as it is revealed in experiences with both overt and more subtle forms of racism in the military. Black Vietnam era veterans talk about conflict with white superiors, being assigned dehumanizing assignments (e.g., cleaning latrines), and tales of racial solidarity among the troops. AVF era veterans describe both successes (e.g., promotion) and unexpected downward spirals as members of the U.S. armed services (e.g., being forced into unexpectedly dangerous combat roles and doing time in the brig).

Chapter 5, The Journey Home, is the book's focal chapter. Here, I look at the complex challenges black veterans experience *after* their careers in the military have ended. Set against a backdrop of racial turmoil, veterans return to various moments in the history of the civil rights movement (e.g., returning to race riots and a city occupied by the National Guard) and post-civil rights decline (e.g., mass incarceration and the war on drugs). This chapter also provides vivid detail of the complex personal and collective challenges African-American veterans confront—namely, a lack of steady employment and poverty; entanglements in the criminal justice system, health care marginality, and the challenges of negotiating the VA; and the pervasive struggle to maintain strong social networks.

In chapter 6, I call attention to how veterans' stories of a decaying communal life over time is consonant with what sociologist Kai Erikson defines as "collective trauma." My argument then extends to a critique of veterans' rights in the lives of black veterans. While most of the respondents use veterans' services, I argue that this use occurs primarily in times of crisis; the VA has little positive impact in the everyday lives of black veterans. Rather than attempt to provide specific policy proposals for reforming the VA, the book concludes by considering how black veterans continue to organize at the grassroots. Specifically, I present the experiences of one African-American veteran with NABVETS.

Taken together *Disposable Heroes* is a call to all Americans. Learning about the detailed life experiences of African-American veterans confronts readers with the importance of a far more expansive dialogue that includes both our devastating wars abroad and the deepening inequalities in health, employment, housing, education, and criminal justice that have come to define our smoldering war at home. We owe it to all veterans and non-veterans to find a real and lasting peace on our home front.

Chapter Two

The African-American Veteran as a Social Problem

Carl: My life is so *in* the past. But as a black man who grew up in the Jim Crow era, I know how being black is always a part of everything. I was called baby killer. But it ain't as blatant today. . . . But I've lived for so long in the 'hood or on the street, so I'm trying not to be part of that lifestyle anymore.

Mel: I grew up at a time when the races pretty much stayed away from each other. But being black I think it is a hell of a lot harder for these kids who live here today. Because they lack what I had—a family that was poor but could love and support me. . . . And I read the papers, if you is black and in the wrong place at the wrong time, you'll get arrested and locked up like nobody's business. . . . But make no mistake, Jack, being a black man in the war and coming home to race riots in the street—where your own friends can't even look you in the eye—you can't just file that shit away, you feel me?

Trey: Shit, I feel chewed up and spat out by the military. There is no doubt in my mind that the way I've been treated is because I'm a black man. I mean I can't work! I can't go to school! So, I'm just drifting around this neighborhood, just another lame ass nigger. Just a thug in society's eyes now, I guess. I've been locked up for three months and now have another case hanging over my head. It's like a bad dream that don't stop. So you tell me about how I view my life!?!? Dog, I'm barely hanging on out here.

How does it feel to be a problem?
—W. E. B. Du Bois, *The Souls of Black Folk* (1903)

The popular story of "broken veterans" is a simplistic tale of mentally unstable individuals who, by their own free will, choose to be on the margins of society. It is a story devoid of attention to policies that have led to profoundly adverse social conditions of racial segregation and poverty. Despite the challenges of a young black veteran such as Trey, for example, continued ghettoization and poverty are not part of the national debate. While nearly every administration since World War II has passed legislation authorizing targeted funds for veteran's benefits, the challenges remain enormous. Yet a black veteran like Jackson (see chapter 1) is considered a "success story" under current policy: he's off the streets and in the U.S. Army Reserves.[1] It is irrelevant in today's so-called post-racial America whether or not Jackson makes barely enough money to survive and lives temporarily in substandard housing in an urban area characterized by a longstanding legacy of white racist policies of spatial exclusion and containment that has deepened black poverty and isolation for generations.

Longstanding social problems such as poverty and health care inequality in the United States are viewed as the dilemmas of individuals rather than questions of reform. Media coverage of these issues often ignores the protracted history of both official and unofficial racist housing practices and zoning ordinances that contain impoverished blacks on the margins of cities all across the United States, instead viewing the living situations of these African Americans as individual choices. Despite deepening unemployment and the continued backlash against racial inclusion (e.g., poverty, unemployment, absentee ownership, and exclusionary zoning ordinances), racially targeted policing and mass incarceration is perversely the appropriate response to the "bad choices" of residents.[2] As sociologists Jason Adam Wasserman, Jeffrey Michael Clair, and Chelsea Platt observe, commenting on the politics of homelessness in the contemporary United States, even those "taking positions considered progressive or sympathetic, nonetheless utilize a conceptual framework of 'being a problem' that matches that of less sympathetic positions."[3] In this book, my aim is then to introduce readers to some of the broader social forces at play in the lives of the African-American veterans I interviewed, as well as to introduce readers to individual veterans to show the nuances of their life stories.

INTRODUCING AFRICAN-AMERICAN VIETNAM ERA VETERANS

The life stories of Vietnam era African-American veterans are nuanced and complex. Both Carl and Mel served in front-line infantry units at the height of the conflagration. When asked at the end of their interviews, "Tell me about how you view your life as an African-American veteran today," Carl (age 64) and Mel (age 63) both began by saying how "lucky" or "blessed" they were to be alive. Both have long struggled with combat-related PTSD. After long battles to receive disability benefits (see chapter 5), they have received extensive treatment from the VA for a myriad of health-related problems. They suffer from clinical depression (both Mel and Carl), diabetes (Carl), hypertension (both Carl and Mel), malaria (Mel), cancer (Mel), drug abuse (Carl), and HIV infection (Carl). While both Carl and, to a lesser degree, Mel struggle to make financial ends meet, they maintain connections to their siblings, ex-spouses, children, and grandchildren. However, their fuller responses are revealing:

Carl: How am I doing as an African-American veteran today? Well, it's hard to separate the past from the present. My life is so *in* the past. But as a black man who grew up in the Jim Crow era, I know how being black is always a part of everything. I was called baby killer. But it ain't as blatant today. . . . But I've lived for so long in the 'hood or on the street, so I'm trying not to be part of that lifestyle anymore. I mean, look at this place, this facility is 99.9 percent black and the whole neighborhood is full of poor blacks. Heck, you're the first white person I've talked to in ages [laughs]! But I don't use race as an excuse. What I'm dealing with now is my own doing. I've avoided the problems the war has created for me for so long that sometimes I don't even realize I'm avoiding things.

Interviewer: How so?

Carl: My drug usage especially became an effective form of self-medication, and I am going to go so far as to say, a way of life. I didn't want to think about a lot of the horrible stuff I experienced in Vietnam. And without realizing it, the negative stuff has caught up with me. It certainly has caused me enough problems in life, even to this very day. But here I am putting all I can muster into recovery. I'm glad I can do it in here and not out there, because out there is a death sentence.

Interviewer: Right, but what about being a grandfather and all?

Carl: Heck, I should be dead [laughs]. But, yeah, I do have so much to live for, like my beautiful relationship with my grandson. He's only 3 years old. He loves me and calls me "best buddy." And I call him "my best buddy." And that's the only thing he knows about me. He's never seen me like a J.A.—that stands for jack ass—in the street or falling down drunk. Actually, a few weeks ago I took him to the zoo for the first time ever—imagine that [shakes his head]—and we had a ball. So that's a huge thing for me, spending quality time with my grandson.

Interviewer: Yeah, you're relationship is so wonderful. But what about living here at Independence House?

Carl: Yeah. . . . I can honestly say that I'm still dealing with a lot of unresolved stuff. . . . None of it will probably ever be fully resolved: Vietnam screwed me up probably for life. But the only difference today is that I want to actually live my life—instead of getting high all the time—and make up for as much lost time as I can. So even though my address is in the 'hood, I have a chance staying inside here to make it. So that's "Carl today" in a nutshell.

Carl's story is a tale of survival in the life of an African-American veteran who is well aware of his challenging surroundings. Perhaps most pervasively is Carl's lack of one of the most taken for granted of white privileges—namely, *having enough time or energy*.[4] Carl's life is one of survival. At the same time, he works to be a loving grandfather who can take his "best buddy" grandson to the zoo. But Carl "struggles with a lot unresolved stuff." In and out of drug rehabs and detoxes for most of his adult life, Carl's current "address is in the 'hood." The broader conditions of marginality—namely, a lack of employment opportunities, housing shortages and deteriorating living conditions, and the neighborhood's street level drug economy—remain an inescapable part of his life. But he tries to stay away from street life. Despite the challenges of his living environment and the continued pains of war that he lives with every day—some four decades after his return from Vietnam—Carl is determined to make a positive recovery.

Interviewer: So, Mel, tell me about how you view your life as an African-American veteran today.

Mel: I grew up at a time when the races pretty much stayed away from each other. But being black I think is a hell of a lot harder for these kids who live here today. Because they lack what I had—a family that was poor but could love and support me. . . . And I read the papers, if you is black and in the wrong place at the wrong time, you'll get arrested and locked up like nobody's business. . . . But make no mistake, Jack, being a black man in the war and coming home to race riots in the street—where your own friends can't even look you in the eye—you can't just file that shit away, you feel me? But I always have been one who tries to see the best in everyone. And as long as I've lived in Wilmington—which is forever [laughs]—I've got white friends and black friends and white enemies and black enemies. . . . But personally today it's my struggle with depression which I have no doubt is the product of being in the 'Nam. How couldn't it be? It was so brutal, man, I could tell you stories. . . . But at least my medications are right and my cancer has been in remission for many years now. And more than in a long time, I constantly feel the urge to get back out on the road and travel.

Interviewer: Oh really, I didn't know you liked to travel?

Mel: Oh, hell yes. Man, there's so much to see beyond this tiny city. I was fortunate to work in many different states after Vietnam, and it was the greatest experience of my life. It gave me a taste for traveling that I have to this day. I plan to take my grandson on a trip, once school is out. . . . But I've got my hands full raising him.

Interviewer: Tell me about it?

Mel: It's very challenging. . . . But, Jack, I went through the 'Nam and a lot of innocent kids were killed for nothing. After that, I'm all about protecting kids. That's my, I mean back in 'Nam you go into the bush and you would see little Vietnamese kids and the first thing we would do is protect them kids, get them the hell out of there. So I'm very protective of all my kids—I have five daughters and a son, they're all grown now—but my grandson, oh my goodness, he's a hyper little son of a gun [laughs]. He's got ADHD. I got him a psychiatrist, dietician, and a counselor. But when I do homework with him, now that's a battle. Me and him fight doing homework. . . . And when he's slacking, I put him on what I call "super punishment." Actually, for six months now I took all the videogames and television out of his room. I let him play out here [living room area] but it's

> real regimented to only certain times. Like I said he's a young black boy in a tough situation, but I got his back. . . . They almost groom kids like him for prison these days. But I got his back. . . . Although, I'd be lying if I didn't say that sometimes it becomes overwhelming for me. I have to go into my little cocoon here. So I'll take him to stay with his aunt for a few days or whatever. But we make it work.

Mel has never had serious problems with alcohol or drugs and lives in a reasonably spacious apartment complex in a lower-working-class neighborhood (e.g., a place not considered in "the 'hood"). His own experience as a black man is most salient in his memories of the past, especially after his return home from Vietnam (e.g., "where your own friends can't even look you in the eye").[5] While he continues to struggle with clinical depression, PTSD, and hypertension, Mel's biggest concern is raising his young black grandson in a city he views as far less forgiving then the one he grew up in. In contrast to Carl, Mel has had a longstanding relationship with his grandson, who has lived with him for many years. Just as his parents raised him, Mel prides himself on taking his grandson's education very seriously. Additionally, Mel has an extensive work history. He has worked and lived in several states across the country—Mel loves to travel and wants his grandson to experience new places away from home. Despite the challenges of being a guardian, Mel is a dedicated care provider. Although Vietnam has left him with emotional and subsequent physical problems—he connects his PTSD to his battle with depression—Mel is somehow able to take strength from his experience in the military. Confronting the awful reality of seeing young children in a war zone, Mel describes coming away from this experience with a different worldview, one he explains as crucial for understanding why he is so "protective" of his grandson today.

AFRICAN-AMERICANS VETERANS OF THE AVF ERA

In their important study of U.S. Army Reservists who served in the Iraq War, Michael Musheno and Susan Ross illuminate in their book, *Deployed: How Reservists Bear the Burden of Iraq*, the steady rise of the post-conscription AVF era. Specifically, they show how the role of reservists and national guardsmen has increasingly been combat-centered, especially after the attacks of September 11, 2001.[6] While their historical overview sheds light on important organizational changes in the military's combat and command structure, it is also important to note that the AVF era comprises numerous combat operations in addition to the more well-known Operation Desert

Storm and the current wars in Iraq and Afghanistan. Soldiers in Honduras and Panama, for example, participated in dangerous combat operations. Moreover, while the AVF era may have until very recently been hidden in the "Shadows of Vietnam," black veterans of this era experience in-service racism, service-related PTSD, and the often punitive and, indeed, dehumanizing experience of being incarcerated in brutal military brigs (see chapter 4).

The AVF era respondents I interviewed served in a diverse array of locations and roles. Three of ten served in combat roles: a Cold War era sniper who served in the jungles of Honduras in the early 1980s and two active duty marines who served in security forces as part of the ongoing Operation Iraqi Freedom. As will become clear, the AVF era is not without racial controversy. First and foremost, it is important to consider the legacy of the Vietnam War and its immediate aftermath on the present. Vietnam played a major role in catalyzing the massive contemporary War on Drugs that has resulted in the veritable decimation of urban communities of color.[7] Michelle Alexander writes in her important book, *The New Jim Crow*:

> [T]he frantic accusations of genocide by poor blacks in the early years of the War on Drugs seem less paranoid. The intuition of those residing in ghetto communities that they had suddenly become *disposable* [emphasis added] was rooted in a real change in the economy—changes that have been devastating to poor black communities as factories have closed, low-skill jobs have disappeared, and all those who had the means to flee the ghetto did. The sense among those left behind that society no longer has use for them, and that the government now aims simply to get rid of them, reflects a reality that many of us who claim to care prefer to avoid simply by changing channels.[8]

The precursor to the new Jim Crow was Nixon's inaugural drug war. While the strategy began with a sweeping public health imperative to "help" Vietnam veterans, it soon gave way to a sweeping law-and-order response targeting low-level street dealers in impoverished communities of color:

> [T]he political needs of the Nixon administration kept intruding—especially as the reelection campaign got under way. . . . An early instance came in 1972, when the White House set up an Office of Drug Law Enforcement (ODALE) to create federal-local strike forces to fight the street-level drug trade in cities across the country. In an election year, though, that did not much matter. "The street pusher program is good politics and has widespread acceptance wherever it's talked about," John Ehrlichman [Nixon advisor] wrote to Nixon on February 8, 1972.[9]

Throughout the 1970s, a volatile white backlash against busing programs aimed at integrating public schools also created profound problems for poor communities of color. Two 51-year-old AVF era black veterans I interviewed were bused from impoverished neighborhoods to schools in more affluent white communities and joined the military after expulsion in the midst of growing racial turmoil and school race riots. In a cruel irony, these black men became defenders of democracy as the result of a profoundly undemocratic period in recent U.S. history. That is to say, their military careers began precisely because of an anti-black ideology that Lillian B. Rubin, quoting Michigan Senator Philip Hart, described in her important book *Busing and Backlash*:

> [T]o insist that the rules of democracy required that school boards be bound by the will of the majority was to deny the oppressive and undemocratic consequences to blacks of that white majority will. More important, it was to fail to grasp that one of the most vexing political problems of late twentieth-century America is not how to ensure majority rule, but how to protect minorities from majority tyranny. Finally, to those critics who insist they oppose busing because it wastes valuable time and does not touch upon fundamental educational problems, I commend the words of Senator Philip Hart of Michigan: "Undoubtedly, a child does not learn arithmetic while riding a bus and busing alone will not insure a quality education, but life will not be very good for the best mathematician if indeed the country is at war within itself when he or she becomes an adult."[10]

In the Reagan era of the 1980s, simultaneously enormous increases in unemployment and aggressive mass incarceration strategies made the military a last escape for many young marginalized black men. More recently, one must also consider the massive cuts in public school funding. The war on public schools has been accompanied by the harsh turn to the so-called school-to-prison pipeline,[11] a situation that has only intensified in the twenty-first century. It is against this backdrop that military recruiters are able to target impoverished communities. This strategy can be seen as part of a de facto "poverty draft." Yet residents in these communities have aggressively contested these efforts:

> One of the more dramatic protests targeting a recruitment station took place in late November of 2004 in Philadelphia. . . . [Protesters] carrying signs that read, "Bring the Money Home" and "Billions for War, Still Nothing for the Poor," briefly took over a recruitment office and issued a list of demands including affordable housing and domestic violence shelters. Several homeless families stated that they had relatives fighting in Iraq.[12]

Consider the experience of a young, impoverished, African-American veteran, Trey (age 26), who recently returned from service in Iraq. Trey "enlisted to get out of the 'hood." As a member of a Marine security force, he was given the harrowing task of having to clear land mines and regularly confront enemy fire. After returning home from more than a year in combat, Trey immediately went absent without leave (AWOL) after telling off a white superior he described as a "racist asshole." This turn of events led to a negative discharge. While data on black Iraq veterans who received bad conduct discharges has not been released, enormous racial disparities among Vietnam veterans of color is well documented, as sociologist Paul Starr uncovered in his scathing Vietnam era tome, *The Discarded Army: Veterans After Vietnam*:

> From the Gulf of Tonkin Resolution in 1964 through the summer of 1972, more than 175,000 soldiers were dismissed with less than honorable discharges. If the reception that other veterans have received has been ambivalent, the homecoming these men have faced has been even more dismal. Were their discharge papers their only handicap, the prospect for these veterans might not be that serious, but typically a bad discharge is only the most recent problem in a biography of misfortune. Often poor, almost always with limited education, disproportionately black, veterans with less than honorable discharges have a series of strikes against them. Employers who have more than enough jobless veterans to choose from will consider these men last and usually not at all.[13]

If Trey's experience is any indication, the impact of receiving a bad conduct discharge in the lives of today's black veterans is devastating. The already marginalized veteran is now profoundly deterred from pursuing employment or veteran's benefits, including GI Bill educational assistance or VA health benefits. When I first met Trey, he had very recently been paroled for drug possession after numerous other entanglements with the criminal justice system since his return. Our interview was comparatively short as Trey was emotionally and physically exhausted. Although he had not seen a physician since returning, he described to me feeling "totally withdrawn" and also suffering from back pain he attributed to a close call with a land mine that never exploded but caused him to violently wrench his back.

Interviewer: Tell me about how you view your life as an African-American veteran today.

Trey: Shit, I feel chewed up and spat out by the military. There is no doubt in my mind that the way I've been treated is because I'm a black man. I mean I can't work! I can't go to school! So, I'm just drifting around this neighborhood just another lame ass nigger. Just a thug in society's eyes now, I guess. I've been locked up for three months and now have another case hanging over my head. It's like a bad dream that don't stop. So you tell me about how I view my life!?!? Dog, I'm barely hanging on out here.

Interviewer: What about your family?

Trey: My mom and grandma love me no matter what. They've stuck by me my entire life. They never have judged me and are proud of my service. But I can see my mama's tears too, you know what I'm saying? She's bottling up so much pain inside. And that hurts me, because I feel like I'm the cause of that. So, it's hard, man. It's real hard.

Interviewer: What about your day-to-day? Is there anything in your life that provides you happiness?

Trey: My family. All my nieces and nephews. I love playing video games with them and what have you. But I'm really into drawing. I do tags for friends I know who rap and stuff like that. I want to be an artist. I mean if I could create and get paid, none of what's going on now in my life would even matter. So I can really get lost when I'm putting ink to paper, you know what I'm saying . . . ? Also, my girlfriend. I was living on the streets actually with other vets I had met in the joint, but I knew her from way back and so now I'm living with her. So, that's cool. She supports me, loves me unconditionally.

Trey's experience in the military turned his civilian life upside down to the point of where he struggles as "a broken black veteran" or what he describes as a "thug" with little to live for. Yet Trey's story isn't entirely devoid of agency. Indeed, he describes strong bonds with his mother, girlfriend, and he dreams one day of becoming a successful artist. Indeed, Trey cannot be easily labeled the "thug" he describes. Instead, like other marginalized black men, Trey's words reveal "a more complex creative actor"[14] who is in constant negotiation with his circumstances no matter how challenging.

Comparing Trey to Carl and Mel is quite instructive. As a much younger veteran, Trey teaches us about the current challenges of being a disenfranchised black male in the United States today. In comparison to Carl and Mel, Trey does not have the experience of being married or having to care for a child or a grandchild. While his story shows the critical importance of his kin networks to his very survival,[15] there is far more uncertainty in Trey's future. Clearly, the drug war and a building criminal record are compounding his problems as a veteran who has received a bad conduct discharge. Trey's life is also far closer to a grown-up version of Mel's grandson. In many ways, Trey represents Mel's fears come true. At the same time, given all Trey has been through as a black veteran, I suspect Mel would be empathetic to Trey (especially when we learn more about Mel's life in subsequent chapters).

UNDERSTANDING THE LIVES OF AFRICAN-AMERICAN VETERANS

In sharing their stories of present day experiences as African-American veterans, respondents describe situations that are not easily separated from either direct experiences with living in racially aggrieved conditions (having to confront challenging racial conditions as they pertain to many aspects of their everyday lives, e.g., having to raise a young, African-American male child in a punitive city, having a criminal record, etc.) or feeling an outright sense of betrayal by the military. I therefore began by presenting black veterans' current experiences in order to highlight both the salience of race and, more importantly, to illuminate the need for a more *expansive inquiry*. In order to understand the perspectives of black veterans today, it is critical to explore their pre- and post-military experiences in detail. Before describing my analytical approach, I want to explain why I did not interview white veterans. My exclusive focus on African Americans is epistemological: as an alternative to the conventional view that the comparison of racial groups is the only way to understand why "race" matters in society, I focus on complex *intra*group differences in the lives of African-American veterans from different generations. In this way, *Disposable Heroes* is not simply a book about one small group of black veterans from the same neighborhood, although I believe that approach is important as well because, with some notable exceptions,[16] much of what we know about poor, urban black men is as criminals.

To study the lives of black veterans is inescapably a study of social mobility and immobility. Since World War II, military service is taken for granted as a catalyst for upward mobility in the lives of African-Americans veterans. Yet important new historical work illuminates how the GI Bill and other veteran benefit programs have not nearly produced the positive impact typically presumed. Glen C. Altschuler and Stuart Blumin make this observation in *The GI Bill: A New Deal for Veterans*, perhaps the most comprehensive social historical account of the GI Bill ever written:

> The GI Bill did indeed provide educational opportunities to millions of women, blacks, and economically disadvantaged veterans that were offered to non-GIs. Many of them subsequently became active in civic and political organizations and helped advance the cause of equal rights in the United States. Nonetheless, as Army Nurse Corps veteran Ann Bertini put it, "They really created it with men in mind, didn't they?" White men, she might have added. With notable exception of Congressman Rankin, the authors and administrators of the bill did not consciously intend the legislation to be racist or sexist. Neither did they challenge dominant assumptions about race and gender in the 1940s or take into account the implications of a benefit conferred exclusively on veterans of the armed forces, a bastion of white privilege.[17]

A primary objective of *Disposable Heroes* is to engage a dialogue on "black veterans" as more than a group of militant thugs, drug dealers, or junkies most often associated with Vietnam era black veterans.[18] African-American veterans have a multiplicity of pre- and post-military experiences. As a veteran and a sociologist of race relations, I therefore am interested in how African-American veterans have *negotiated* their lives over time, especially since returning to an often unforgiving civilian environment. Attending to their life experiences illuminates both the pains of war abroad and at home, and indeed, in a society still profoundly characterized by racial inequalities and "structural violence."[19]

The stories of Jackson, Carl, Mel, Trey, Joe, and numerous other African-American veterans presented in this book illuminate complex lives not easily separated from their significantly *less* privileged positions in life as marginalized black men. In the accounts I've presented so far, references to challenging racial conditions both before and after the war provide important clues into the lives of African-American veterans. Jackson's unstable living situation and lack of a strong social network, Joe's struggle to embrace the VA after lengthy service in Iraq, Carl's decades of post-war struggles and the current challenges of life in a racially aggrieved neighborhood, and Trey's bad conduct discharge and subsequent difficult post-military experiences as a young black man all foreshadow individual and collective struggles not easily separated from persistent racial matters. Likewise, Mel's story illuminates a resilient, albeit challenging situation as a 62-year-old man charged with raising a young grandson in a city that is increasingly unforgiving to young black men.

Only knowing about answers to the question "Tell me about how you view your life as an African-American veteran today" in many ways raises more questions than answers. That is to say, these men's stories of their present experiences beg for a more detailed exploration of their pre- and post-military lives. How did they decide to join the military in the first place? What kind of experiences did they have in the service? What has happened in their lives since the time they returned from the service? My approach to these questions is less a search for particular answers. Instead, my life history approach is indebted to the remarkable and grossly overlooked work of the late black sociologist Charles S. Johnson. His seminal books *Shadow of the Plantation* (1934), *Growing Up in the Black Belt* (1941), and *Patterns of Negro Segregation* (1943) employed a rich life history approach with specific attention to post-slavery trauma in the lives of rural blacks and their communities. What is notable in all of Johnson's empirical research is precisely the fascinating historical parallels he draws between, for example, early systems of enslavement to contextualize experiences of former black slaves and their children. As one of the earliest students of the Chicago School of Sociology, Johnson's approach stands out for his willingness to be critical of sociology's invariably narrow approach—namely, most empirical research is preoccupied with explaining black criminality with far less attention to broader sociohistorical conditions. Johnson's work is perhaps the first to present rich life stories of black respondents with explicit attention to slavery and continuing conditions of white oppression.[20]

Following Johnson, my analysis of African-American veterans makes *explicit* the history of white oppression that has resulted in dramatically constrained opportunities. I present the experiences of individuals with attention to broader and often unstable conditions of racial inequality. This requires attention to a history that extends back to slavery and a systematic backlash against Black Reconstruction and the struggle to enforce greater racial inclusivity and genuine citizenship ever since.[21] To be sure, there have been unprecedented legal reforms implemented since the end of America's Civil War, including additional amendments to the U.S. Constitution that extended fundamental legal rights to blacks such as the right to vote. In the decades since Black Reconstruction, the U.S. Supreme Court has issued several landmark decisions in the pursuit of equal rights for African-Americans. Brown v. Board of Education of Topeka (1954) struck down the longstanding "separate but equal" doctrine as it applied to education. And the landmark Shelley v. Kramer (1948) declared racist practices in urban housing such as "block busting" and "racial steering" unconstitutional. In recent decades, a more conservative U.S. Supreme Court has taken a far more "hands off" approach to furthering the struggle for civil rights. The cumulative impact has been continued ghettoization of blacks and an attendant lack of access to quality education, suitable housing, and employment opportunities.[22]

Yet when social scientists conduct longitudinal research on inequality it is invariably *ahistorical* (e.g., the idea that today racial segregation in housing has ended). With some notable exceptions,[23] empirical research focuses on turning points in respondents lives with little attention to policy regimes or broader social conditions that cannot be easily separated from other social problems (e.g., poverty and unemployment). Many life history scholars also study the impact of *social capital* (e.g. financial and human resources, strong social networks, and cultural experiences that positively impact an individual's worldview) with little attention to how broader structural conditions of inequality and marginality impact the lives of respondents. The focus on social capital also tends to lack clarity. Alford R. Young Jr., in his important study of marginalized African-American men living on Chicago's Near West Side provides an important critique and refinement:

> There are gains and losses in making use of a broad term like *capital*. The fact that it can be applied simultaneously to so many objects and ideas makes it a useful construct for creating a leveled analytical field. . . . On the other hand,

> the breadth of the term *capital* renders it problematic as an analytical *construct* [emphasis added]. One runs the risk of lacking coherence and focus when employing it to explain the relevant factors for a social phenomenon or occurrence. . . . [S]ocial capital has a two-fold definition. On one hand, social capital depends on the degree to which an individual is imbedded in social networks that can bring about the rewards and benefits that enhance his or her life. In this way, social capital is seen as a precursor to the acquisition of other forms of capital (money, information, social standing, etc.). On the other hand, social capital has been identified as the package of norms and sanctions maintained by groups so that positive or desired outcomes occur for all members, especially those that no single member could achieve on his or her own.[24]

The study of social capital is therefore most clearly attended to *dialectically*. How an individual negotiates the life course is never a clean linear process. Various events—in the case of veterans, for example, individually and collectively traumatizing experiences—create both open and blocked opportunities not simply for or by individuals but in concert or in tension with broader social relations. For example, veterans' benefits may provide enough financial capital to afford an apartment but a subsequent divorce may result in both emotional upheaval and the insurmountable burden of keeping up with child support payments. Yet such a situation may not last if, for example, a veteran reconciles with a spouse and/or is able to use the GI bill to become more socially mobile. At the same time, with increased racially targeted drug war policing, a veteran struggling with addiction might suddenly become ensnared in the criminal justice system thereby severing the financial capital provided previously by veteran's benefits.

It is equally important to attend to the *social deficits* experienced by African-American veterans at various periods in their lives. Beyond the loss of financial capital, such a line of inquiry necessarily involves attending to traumatic events that may appear to begin and end with the individual. However, as I noted in the book's introduction, early traumatic experiences may quickly take on a collective character in which veteran's broader social networks are profoundly compromised, leaving them sometimes quite literally to fend for the themselves. When viewed across various stages of one's life history, the struggle to survive that is so pervasive in the lives of marginalized African-American veterans takes on a distinctly cumulative character. To reiterate, this is not to imply a linear trajectory—indeed, as we will see, the life experiences presented here are often cyclical and, indeed, unpredictable. The main thrust of my argument is that studying African-American veterans' lives is best understood in a broad, historically dynamic context.

Chapter Three

Joining Up

Lionel: I was drafted into Vietnam. So I had no choice. I just accepted that this was the normal course of life. I mean, there were no expectations that you wouldn't be drafted. And getting drafted was a ticket out of the ghetto. So the military draft just became another thing black men had to deal with. We were kind of in our own space, in our own place, and dealt with things that affected our own surroundings. I mean you knew if you went across the tracks, you'd have to deal with Jim Crow, so you just stayed away. But going into the military was almost a rite of passage for those that were physically fit, unless you had some kind of deferment, the bottom line was this: you were gonna go.

Gerald: I got kicked out of high school at the end of my senior year in '78 for felonious assault. There was this white kid who I would hang out with and I was in the library—I loved to read and would be late to class—and when I got out I see these two other white kids beating up my friend and calling him nigger lover. I mean it's two against one, so I jumped in and beat the hell out of both them. And, of course, the cops come and I was forced to either face the charges or take an expulsion. . . . So then I got my GED and ended up enlisting in the air force, but it all happened so quick.

Andre: Because I wanted to be the best, I wanted to be looked at as honorable. I mean my cousins were active duty in the army at the time, but I really did not pay them any attention whatsoever. I mean, I knew I wanted to do something *extra* ordinary. Ever since I was a kid I wanted go to the NFL, but I never excelled

> enough to play in the NFL or even college ball. So I thought hard about that, and well, I decided I'll be a Marine. And I enlisted in the Delayed Entry Training (DET) program my senior year, so I actually still had a chance to get out because of course if you're in the DET program you're not all the way enlisted—you can out and do something else if you want to. But then 9/11 happened; I thought what happened was so horrible. And I was already half way into the Marine Corps, said I'll go over to Iraq and kick some of their butts for what they did.

These men were responding to my question about what led them to join the military. Each represents a different generation from the Vietnam and AVF eras. Lionel (age 68) grew up in a large Baltimore housing project before being drafted. Gerald is a "cold war warrior" who joined the air force after a tumultuous year of race riots that occurred in the midst of white backlash towards the busing of poor, urban, black youth to suburban, predominantly white high schools. Andre (age 28) enlisted in the Marine Corps' DET but formally enlisted after the attacks on the World Trade Center twin towers on September 11, 2001. Their different pathways into the military, like those of other African-American veterans, cannot be understood without attending to their childhood and other formative experiences. This observation, I believe, holds for both their in-service and post-service phases of their lives as well.

It is tempting to focus in on particular turning points in the lives of African-American veterans. However, I believe, as the above accounts suggest, that it is at the *interface* of key life experiences and broader contexts of poverty and marginality that is most illuminating. It was in the course of multiple individual, institutional, and structural contexts where we learn about how African-American veterans make sense of their lives. To this end, I do not seek to show how the presence or absence of a father figure, to take one particularly common place for analysis, leads to particular outcomes in their lives. Instead, I stay as close to the men's words as possible to understand how their past experiences framed subsequent turning points in their lives. This approach is consistent with a recent comprehensive overview of quantitative studies of the impact of military service on the life course that called for greater attention to "social context, the forces that impel people to serve in the military, the political factors that shape the military experience and the opportunities afforded to service members during and after their tours of duty."[1]

I also pay less explicit attention to war stories, both figuratively and literally, but instead attend to how particular experiences at home, in the service, and post-service illustrate African-American veterans' experiences at various points in their lives. For half of the respondents I interviewed, the constrained world of an inner city transitional housing program in many ways *is* their social world. The choices that these African-American veterans made led them on paths of extreme downward mobility. However, as previous research confirms, not all of them are chronically homeless, indeed most of the veterans I interviewed at IH had only recently experienced life in the absence of steady housing. The other fifteen veterans I interviewed also live to varying degrees in marginalized urban communities. Some live in housing conditions that are in many ways worse than IH. They live in overcrowded and deteriorating housing conditions in the midst of sometimes extreme conditions of social deprivation, including chronic unemployment, open-air drug markets, and aggressive police presence. Indeed, only two of the respondents I interviewed lived in what can be considered edge communities that are somewhat spatially buffered from the more marginalized neighborhoods.

ACCOUNTING FOR BELIEFS

> *What* man is may be so entangled with *where* he is, *who* he is, and *what he believes* [emphasis added] that it is inseparable from [him or her].
>
> —Clifford Geertz, *The Interpretation of Cultures* (1973)

Current situations shape the way African-American veterans view their pasts and how they subsequently characterize their prospects for the future. Indeed, most respondents I interviewed travel outside their current surroundings only if they are accessing the VA services. Although some describe positive experiences beyond treatment—gaining access to financial capital in the form of access to disability, heath benefits, and even the GI Bill—most respondents use the VA as an option of last resort (e.g., a health crisis). Despite the fact that the military has afforded them the opportunity to have left their current surroundings, many respondents are now estranged from the outside world, as their lives are rooted in the pains of the present and what they perceive to be a future characterized by struggle. African-American veterans' lives have far more to do with surviving than yellow ribbon parades or any other popular symbolism of the war hero. We begin with an exploration of Vietnam era veterans' pre-military experiences. These individual stories reveal deeper connections to collective experiences. Attending to veterans' pre-military experiences then provides an important way to foreground experiences in the military (see chapter 4) and their subsequent struggles on the home front (see chapter 5).

JIM CROW IN THE EARLY LIVES OF VIETNAM VETERANS: "THERE REALLY WASN'T ANY CHOICE."

Lionel (age 66) was raised in a large East Baltimore housing project where he grew up with his mother and sister. When asked about whether he remembers any explicitly racist experiences, he explains: "Well, yeah, I grew up in Jim Crow segregation. And we were on social services and we experienced unannounced late night raids to make sure no one else was living there. It was crazy back then." Lionel expounds on such "crazy times":

> When we went downtown there were certain stores you couldn't go into, you couldn't try anything on. You couldn't try on clothes. Certain business you could only enter through the back door. There were certain parks that were Jim Crow that we couldn't go to. There were days when it was "only white" or "only black" and you could never mix the two. And most of the families were like mine: kids with young mothers but very few had fathers. Out of the whole project you had like five. . . . I mean ten [fathers] is a stretch. I mean you got to realize having a father present in the household was frowned upon back in those days. If you had a man living in the household bringing in income, you wouldn't qualify for a lot of the social programs that they had back then.

Terrifying midnight raids of black families by white Aid to Dependent Children (ADC) agents was commonplace during this era. The history of these dehumanizing practices is well documented.[2] In addition to growing up in overtly racially oppressive housing conditions, Lionel recalls confronting neighbors—young black veterans recently back from duty in Vietnam—who had suffered both serious psychological and physical injuries:

> We had one guy living in the project who was shell shocked—word on the street was he was shell shocked from being in the war. And then as the Vietnam War began, we had friends who would go over there and come back. Some would come back maimed, with no arms or legs. . . . It was real tough. . . . But if you weren't immediately impacted—if it wasn't your family member—if you weren't bothered, you had to just press on. I mean we were all close, but it was a time of war, so there really wasn't any choice.

Lionel's words illuminate how Vietnam made an already oppressive living situation for blacks in a racially hostile housing project a multi-layered collective trauma that was not simply episodic but part of a larger black communal experience. Throughout the interview Lionel was very lucid and spoke calmly even when describing such difficult experiences. It is clear that because he had not lived in these oppressive conditions for decades it is much easier for him to speak about them today. Moreover, as we will see in the next chapter, Lionel's more recent financial challenges in all likelihood make talking about his pre-military years seem like a distant memory. But it is clear that African-American veterans experience traumatic experiences that serve to rupture stability in community life. While most of the veterans I interviewed did not serve in combat, nonetheless their pre- and post-military experiences are deeply rooted in broader conditions of racial oppression and trauma that outstrip many of the positive impacts of service reported by sociologists,[3] especially when they try to adjust to a civilian life that for many has become qualitatively worse.

The Vietnam era, as has been richly documented,[4] occurred in a period in American history characterized by dramatic social upheaval and increased upward mobility for many blacks, including those who served in the military. Yet attending to the life experiences of African-American veterans of this period reveals a myriad of challenges that cannot easily be reconciled by implicit assumptions of racial progress. Indeed, the *cumulative* aspect of individual and collective traumas in their lives reveals an amalgam of challenges that span pre-service, service, and post-service experiences. I begin with an exploration of Vietnam era veterans' pre-military experiences and then turn to AVF era veterans.

"WE WERE LIVING IN THE SHADOWS"

When I first met Carl (age 64), the decorated Vietnam veteran I introduced in the previous chapter, I was admittedly shocked by his physical appearance. He was bone thin and had sunken cheeks. Carl's hands trembled throughout our entire interview. He is infected with the HIV virus—which he treats with a strict regimen of anti-retroviral medication—but given his lack of muscle mass, it seems likely that he is not getting enough nutritional supplementation in his diet. In a previous book, I studied hundreds of pages of medical mortality reviews, and Carl's appearance seems to reveal dangerous signs of neglect. However, I cannot be certain of this observation as a non-physician, nor was I given access to his voluminous and detailed medical history.

But one thing is certain: Carl was very eager to talk about his life on the multiple days I interviewed him and also his ex-wife, Pauline (see chapter 5). As soon we began to talk it was quite clear that he is both very lucid and has a detailed recall of his early life history. Carl began our interview with a wide smile and said, "What is a professor like you doing out here in the 'hood [laughs]?" After talking a little bit about my own experience in the service, he informed me that he was eager to talk, "because I haven't had a good conversation with anybody in weeks [laughs]!" Despite my concerns about his health, we immediately developed a strong rapport. Indeed, he spoke with ease as he began describing his childhood in an impoverished, racially segregated community in the rural South in the midst of the Jim Crow era.

Carl grew up in abject rural poverty in a small town in Maryland. His father passed away at a very early age, and he grew up the son of a single mother. Like so many black women of this era, Carl's mother did arduous domestic work cleaning the houses of middle class whites for dollars a day. Carl describes a deep love and devotion for his mother, whom he looks back at fondly as "this amazing lady. She worked herself to the bone but came home to us with nothing but love. I don't remember her ever even raising her voice once to me or my sister." Struggling to help his family make ends meet, Carl dropped out of high school in the eleventh grade and took a difficult job working the graveyard shift in a Campbell's soup factory. As a member of the "clean-up crew," Carl and three other young black men "scrubbed every inch of the place." While describing the drudgery of this unforgiving work environment, Carl reflected back on his difficult decision to leave school: "I was a decent student and enjoyed reading, and here I am in this dead end job, so these were hard times." But in hindsight, Carl knew it was the only choice he could make—one based on survival—and he was not "getting the best of education 'cuz the schools and everything else was all segregated when I was coming up."

Another Vietnam era veteran, Delbert (age 66), had a similar experience and provides a concise reflection on these challenges:

Delbert: What people don't understand about Vietnam in the life of the black man during this time is that we were just trying to survive. We were living in the shadows. It was you and your family and friends and your neighborhood and that was it. We weren't wandering across any tracks like they show in movies; you get killed that way.

Interviewer: Before you enlisted, were you going to school and working?

Delbert: I dropped out of school in the tenth grade to make some extra money. I was sick of being broke. It was as simple as that. So, I got a job at a grocery store. Believe it or not, back then that was a pretty good job for a teenager! I'd get hams and stuff to bring home [laughs]. We was living pretty good.

Interviewer: So when you were drafted, did you ever consider trying to get out of going to Vietnam?

Delbert: Yeah, well that crosses the mind, "Go fight in another dumb war." But on the other hand, we was so dirt poor that the service was the only show in town. So when they drafted me I was ready. I became the best damned killer that this man's army could produce. That's why I reenlisted and did another tour; there was some money and I had the best training around serving in the infantry, so I was ready.

Interviewer: Did you ever consider joining the National Guard?

Delbert: Back then? Shit . . . The guard was a white man's outfit. They ain't signing up no niggers. And looking back, I'm glad I stayed away from the guard altogether because guess who was running the show back home? Right, the National Guard had occupied the city. But I missed all that because I reenlisted and did another tour in 'Nam.

"IT WAS ONE BIG RUSH"

Alternatively, other black veterans describe their early years in terms of strong kin networks and access to educational capital. Mel (age 63) remembers being "racially segregated and dirt poor, but we took pride in our neighborhood. We had nice lawns, no garbage spilling out like you see all over the city today. I remember tearing around the streets with my buddies on our bikes until it was dark. My kids and grandkids could never do that kinda stuff today, especially with the drugs and what not." Although they struggled to make ends meet, both of Mel's parents worked and his many relatives were always around the family home. Mel also credits his father with introducing him to jazz music: "My dad was an 'easy going cat.' He loved Charlie Parker, Miles, all that great stuff. And he also played the horn and had musicians around the house from time to time." Although he describes himself as the black sheep of the family, education was always a top priority in Mel's life: "My folks always really stressed education. If I came home with a C, put it this way: I wasn't coming home with a C again! [laughs]. The B or B+ range was cool but anything in the C range wasn't cool enough. Both my parents and my aunts, who were all teachers, always stressed that my brothers and sisters and I could always do better." Mel went to an African-American high school he described as having "great teachers and coaches. I mean, all of them were supportive and encouraged you to dream big."

Mel's early childhood sheds light on his resilience today. He is able to provide for his grandson (see chapter 2) and tries to instill the educational discipline and cultural capital of his early years. In addition to the video games, there were several horns in his living room and jazz was playing on the stereo throughout our interview. He wants his grandson to "be a dreamer and never settle. . . . Music is a powerful way for him to come into his own. I just want to expose him to the rich tradition of jazz that I grew up with and maybe music will be his thing. I ain't pushing it but want him to be exposed in the way I was growing up."

Given his childhood, I just assumed Mel was drafted. In high school, Mel described himself as an athlete and an honor student. His decision to enlist in the Marine Corps was like many other respondents: inspired by family members who had served. In this case, Mel's older cousins: "They were twins and I used to love it when they came home just, you know, seeing them in their dress blue uniforms. I admired their service and just planned to go to OCS [Officer's Candidate School] all along. I wanted to be a pilot." And despite the fact that his dreams of being a pilot were dashed after he was assigned to the 3rd Marines Infantry Division with "a ticket straight to the front lines of Vietnam, my parents were very cordial and the vibe from them was nothing but love and support." And echoing Carl's excitement at a chance to see the world, Mel described the days before leaving: "It was one big rush. A journey into a place that was about as far from here as you could get."

"I ALREADY WANTED OUT"

Earl (age 61) grew up the oldest of four children. His appearance was memorable for the military jacket he wore and deep scar on his cheek. Like Carl, Earl showed physical signs of poor health. Throughout our interview, he chain smoked and coughed deeply. At the time of our interview, Earl had moved out of IH. Our interview took place just around the corner from a shelter he was living in, on a bench under a sidewalk bus stop canopy. Before our interview, I bought him a cup of coffee, because he "was tired, real tired. I've had trouble sleeping on the new meds the VA prescribed me." Despite being obviously exhausted, Earl was still eager to talk about his experiences. When I asked about where he grew up in the city, Earl pointed his finger and stated, "Just around the corner from that convenience store." After a brief walk, I saw the tiny row home in which he and his four siblings were raised. "Yeah, we were pretty squeezed in there, but we made it work. My aunt raised us because I was molested by my mom when I was six years old and my dad was a drunk and never around." The home was located in a section of the city that a local housing authority report described as "filled with numerous abandoned houses." I asked Earl if it was a poor, black neighborhood when he was growing up: "Well, yeah, it was completely segregated by race, but back then nobody messed with anybody, and I went to a Catholic high school." I asked if the church played a big role in his upbringing: "Oh yeah, religion was very big. I actually was an altar boy, believe it or not [laughing]. Yep, a homeless fool like me was an angel back then. I mean the nuns were tough, very strict, but I have nothing but good feelings towards them and my school. They really instilled in us a strong moral foundation." At the same time, the mid-1960s was becoming a time of immense uncertainty in the black community.

Interviewer: What was the community's relationship with police like back then?

Earl: The police were very tough on us. I mean we didn't see them as much as I do now. But I learned very early on to fear the police. I mean whenever we interacted with the police they downgraded you. When the cops came they'd tell us to get off the sidewalk or we're gonna lock you up. Oh yeah, and I remember being terrified, I mean scared shitless, when they would let the police dogs out. Shit, I never ran so fast in my life [laughs]!

Interviewer: Was the community's attitude beginning to change with the civil rights movement?

Earl: We were angry about the economy. But people in my neighborhood, we all had to put the blinders on. I mean it was until after King was gunned down, and I came home that things really began to change. And then the riots broke out and people were running all through the streets. I didn't understand it. But by then my own view had changed. I mean the National Guard is riding with the police all around us. If I remember correctly, let me see, they were dug in around the block from us. And the message was clear to me: you are not welcome on this earth as a black person. And on the TV there was the KKK and the Jim Crows—that's all there was—and during the riots we were pretty much locked inside watching that stuff. It seemed like that's all there was on TV.

After Earl graduated from high school he got a job at the local power company before enlisting. It was on the job that he first encountered employment discrimination, a situation that directly influenced his decision to skip the draft and enlist:

> I was so angry because no matter how hard I worked, I never got a raise. Here, I am a high school graduate, smart and always willing to work overtime. This was like a dream job for me! But they had it in for me because of my race. I should have listened and never taken that job. You see the other black workers told me not to expect ever be promoted. So when I was going to get drafted, I already wanted out, so I went to the recruiter and enlisted.

Despite being molested by his mother at an early age, Earl describes his religious faith as key to his survival. At the same time, the tumultuous times characterizing the 1960s created a profound fear of the police and a sense of racial inferiority. Yet Earl adapted as best he could: he graduated from a good high school and secured gainful employment. It was the workplace for Earl that, in a cruel irony, was the breaking point for him. While it is likely he would not have escaped the draft, Earl enlisted in the military only after his "dream job" fell apart because of workplace discrimination.

"I WANTED SOME CONTROL OF WHAT I'D BE DOING IN THE MILITARY"

My initial plan was to meet Otis (age 65) at IH; however, after several scheduling conflicts due to various legal and health problems he was experiencing with unpaid child support and a chronic cough that became a serious respiratory infection, he was now living in his cousin's basement. Throughout our interview, Otis had to take several breaks to stand. Like Jackson, he also suffered from swollen legs and tooth loss as a result of untreated diabetes. I asked him early on in our interview how he was holding up: "It's, well, business as usual, really." When I asked him to elaborate, Otis tersely explained:

> This is how been for me for so many years, I've forgotten any other way. . . . There's always shit stirred up. Whether it's my health or being broke or having to move out of somewhere. At least, I'm not in the joint! Shit, I've done enough time in there to know that's a death sentence, especially at my age. They'd just let me rot if I went back now. So it's always, always a challenge, you know what I'm saying, Jack? The VA cleans me up and sends me on my merry way. But with all my health issues—diabetes, hypertension, the cigarettes or what have you—it just part of my routine. I wouldn't wish all I've been on anyone, but it is what is. The best thing now is my cousin is always working—two, three jobs or what have you—so I can just be on my own and rest and read the bible. At my age, that's a gift, you know? No one messes with me; I can just be left alone. When shit is stirring up it's "do this, do that," "take this medicine, take that, don't do this, don't do that." It gives me a headache talking about it, actually.

Despite the difficulty of his present situation, Otis's enthusiasm carried over into his story of his early life experiences and decision to join the military. As the "baby" of the family, Otis grew up with two older sisters he describes as "very protective and loving. They'd do anything for me. And to this day we are very, very close." Both of Otis's parents worked to support the family in a neighborhood in the height of Jim Crow segregation. Otis's mother, like so many others of this era, cleaned houses as a domestic worker and his father, a World War II veteran, worked in construction. Otis describes the neighborhood businesses as all white owned. But beyond taking stock of his surroundings, Otis took away a lasting impression of his father's experience as a decorated World War II veteran who grew up in the Jim Crow South: "My father was a very proud man. He grew up in the heart of Jim Crow in South Carolina. But I'll always remember what he told me from a very young age: "If I ever hear you call a white man 'sir,' I'm gonna beat you."

Interviewer: Was he hard on you growing up?

Otis: Yeah, but he always meant well. He just had a problem with alcohol and would go off on us from time to time. . . . I'm almost sure it was the war. He didn't talk too much about it. But given my own experiences later, I'm also certain he suffered from PTSD.

In describing his mother's views about race growing up, Otis was quite blunt: "My mother didn't say much at all about race. I mean she didn't have time! She worked very, very hard and her primary goal was to raise us. I loved her to death." Faith and family also played an important role in Otis's early socialization: "Every day growing up my mom, sisters, and I would sit down and pray and laugh together. I feel truly blessed for that."

Otis also describes his family as very serious about education: "I was a great student. I loved school. My mother made learning and going to school fun for us. I mean, you are not going to bring a C home, that was not an option, but she made it fun for me, she really did." In high school, Otis developed a love of technology and particularly early computer programming. After high school graduation, he worked for a year for a corporation, but as the draft began, "I decided I wanted some control of what I'd be doing in the military, so I enlisted."

However, when I asked Otis if the impending draft was the main reason he enlisted, he explained, "I mean it was part of my strategy. But I wanted to do something. I was the baby of the family, so I just wanted to grow up and do something, instead of having it so easy. But going to Vietnam was devastating for my mom and sisters. They knew that I was going to be alright. Although, they just couldn't understand why I enlisted, but I wanted to be in control of my options. I didn't want to be drafted. I wanted to keep my options open." Otis decided to enlist with a lifelong friend who also wanted to avoid the draft. Hoping that they might stay together in Vietnam, however, didn't come to fruition: "Unfortunately, his test scores weren't as good as mine—I got into data processing, and he was sent into the infantry—so we were separated pretty quick after enlisting."

Interviewer: That must have been hard to have that plan not work out for you?

Otis: Yeah, but he made it back alive too! Man, we sometimes see each other around town and what have you. But he's still plugging away. Although a nasty alcoholic, so I got to keep some distance, especially now that I'm clean and sober.

Interviewer: Does your friend still suffer from the war?

Otis: Oh yeah, he's got PTSD. He lost a lot of friends over there. So that pain's been festering in him for like forty years now. He's had a couple close calls—heart attacks and what have you—but as far as I know, he's still pushing on.

"I WAS DRAFTED—NEXT STOP, VIETNAM"

When I finally found Charles's (age 61) home, I was immediately struck at the deplorable conditions of his neighborhood. My GPS lost its signal as I snaked through what seemed like an endless array of one-way streets that eventually took me to an almost hidden set of decaying housing projects tucked far behind a large highway overpass. I had driven along that highway several times before, but didn't see Charles's neighborhood because it *could not* be seen. Indeed, the only way to Charles's home is to go on a mission and find it. I had read about the neighborhood as "one of the city's worst" but had no idea just how deteriorated the housing was and how tightly wedged in everything was; the place was downright claustrophobic. The apartment Charles and his family lived in was part of a large square of free-standing gray concrete boxes; like the other projects I had seen in Wilmington's most impoverished sections of the city, the entire row of apartments was stained with a kind of black soot that must have gathered over generations of neglect.

Surrounding the projects were several boarded up buildings that, according to Charles, were recently condemned by the city for renovations. But as a lifelong resident of the neighborhood and surrounding area, Charles was much more skeptical about any changes in the quality of housing: "Since the 80s they always say renovations, renovations, renovations. But I've never seen any serious workers rebuilding here. In fact, the only thing I've seen, and this has been more recently, is demolition. You see (pointing down the street) that blank patch of land over there? [I nod.] That used to be a project where some friends I know lived. Now they're living on the other side in their cousin's place." Coming to Charles's house was as visceral an experience with urban racial oppression as I have ever had. In addition to the awful housing conditions, black people slept on street corners or wandered aimlessly on the sidewalks. Once inside Charles's apartment, his son greeted me in a thoroughly cramped front living room. The entire first floor was no more than thirty feet long and ten feet wide. We conducted the interview in his tiny kitchen at a table with a large metal cooking tray stacked high with raw chicken wings that looked as though they would serve at least two, perhaps, three meals worth of food. From the time our interview began to its conclusion, I could see over Charles's shoulder a young, haggard-looking black man with an expressionless look on his face walking in circles around the project's clothesline-filled backyard.

Charles grew up in conditions not too dissimilar from his present situation. The housing project of his birth was a tight squeeze for four people, but Charles grew up living in a space packed with ten people. He described having a very close relationship with his parents. But his father's alcoholism made things very hard on an already oppressive living situation: "He'd always come in late and wake us up yelling and hollering."

Interviewer: What was the neighborhood like back then?

Charles: It was all black but more working class. My mother worked, but we received public assistance because of the size of our family. She worked in a nursing home and prior to that she did house work, cleaning houses as a domestic worker. My dad was a maintenance man but he lost his job. I'm not sure if it was because of his drinking. But things changed for me.

Interviewer: How so?

Charles: I picked that up at a young age, because I got put into foster care at an early age.

Interviewer: Okay, how did that happen?

Charles: Yeah, my mom had so many kids, and people living there, so the state had me move out. They put me in a foster home. I mean, my mom and dad were so poor. I remember in the mornings before I went to school I used to go to ask my mom, "Do you want anything, do you want some coffee this morning, do you want me to run to the store?" And she would say "yeah" and give me a nickel, because a nickel carried a lot of weight in them days. And I would take that nickel and that was my lunch money for school, so when I got to school I wouldn't feel ashamed like I had no lunch money. I had to get a token from the teacher to get a meal, so that was my way of getting lunch money.

Interviewer: Sounds like you did whatever it took to survive?

Charles: Oh yeah, still am [laughs]. But back then people who lived around the corner from us got to liking me and told my mother that they'd like to do something for me. And my mom, she went through a foster agreement. I was too young to know what was going on, but they agreed to raise me.

Charles was fortunate in that his foster parents were extremely supportive. Moreover, his new home was just around the corner from his birth mother's apartment, and his foster parents allowed him to maintain a relationship with his birth family. Charles explains:

> I'm going to tell you first about my foster parents. They were great. They'd take me to state fairs and stuff like I never experienced before. I mean, I never went nowhere, you know? They let me go around the corner some nights when they'd go away and stay with my mom back. And I had a portable TV in my own bedroom. It was quite an experience with my own brothers and sisters, because we were like, you know, crowded in like sardines there. Because we grew up in like a one bedroom apartment. A one bedroom apartment with eight kids! But once I moved in with my new family, I started getting good grades. My foster parents were serious about education but not harsh. So all of the sudden the teachers are telling me that I'm a very bright young man. I still got my report card somewhere buried around here. I save that kinda stuff.

Charles was a decent student all throughout high school. And then his draft number was called for Vietnam. During this time, there was a lot of resistance to the war in the neighborhood:

> Okay, in that period of time we had people like Rap Brown and Stokely Carmichael, those kinda guys that was trying say how we supposed to act, like I "don't take no shit from this guy or that guy," you know, that type of mentality right. So, I grew up around that, and I told my mom, "I'm not going in the service. I'm not going, I'm going to Canada. And you know, she begged me to go because my mom, she was a straight up person. She was like, "All you'll do is bring harm to us, why don't you just go ahead, God gonna bless you." So to one of my boys I said, "Man, you going nigga?" I was like "Shoot, I'm going." So I was drafted—next stop, Vietnam.

Charles's path to Vietnam is interesting on at least two accounts. First, he grew up in abject poverty, barely able to scrape enough change together for lunch money. But a sudden turn of events that led him into foster care was a dramatic turning point in his early childhood. While other veterans described a similar experience of being uprooted from their birth parents at an early age, only Charles described this experience as a dramatic change for the better. He describes his foster parents as extremely supportive and eager to show him a life outside of the projects. Charles is also one of the few black veterans whose exposure to black radicalism of the time had an impact on his pre-service experience. But in the end, and this will be a common theme in subsequent chapters that analyze Charles's post-military experience, his mother had a strong influence on his life. Indeed, she persuaded him not to go AWOL.

RACIAL BACKLASH AND THE DRUG WAR IN THE LIVES OF POST-VIETNAM ERA VETERANS: "WHEN THE CRAP HIT THE FAN"

Gerald (age 51), a "cold-war warrior" is currently unemployed and living in an apartment with his cousin not too far from a downtown college campus. The interview was conducted in an unoccupied classroom that I was able to reserve. Immediately I was struck by Gerald's intelligence. He had a wealth of knowledge, especially on the topics of African-American history and the civil rights movement. I began by asking Gerald about the neighborhood he grew up in: "I mean it wasn't the ghetto. We came up pretty nice. I mean everybody knew everybody and hung out with everybody. Probably the most criminal activity we had was the street lottery or playing the numbers." Gerald's parents were divorced at an early age, but he stayed in contact with his father. He lived with his mother, aunt, and grandmother.

Interviewer: What were your mom and grandmother like?

Gerald: They were all political radicals. Second generation Garveyites, in fact.

Interviewer: Fascinating. What was it like being raised by black nationalists?

Gerald: It was a total lifestyle. By the time I was six I could tell you who Fredrick Douglas and Harriet Tubman were. My mother would walk me over to my grandmother's house and she would question me: "Who started Black History Month?" I mean you needed to know your stuff.

Indeed, as a young man, Gerald recalls attending many demonstrations, including one with his grandmother and sister that was particularly memorable to him:

> There's one incident that stands out in my mind. There was a girl that was there who was same age as I was that had got killed for picking a peach out of a man's tree. And the guy chased these kids down and shot and killed one of them, and what I can remember, there was a chance that he wasn't going to be charged with murder. Actually, he was not charged with murder, he was charged with a manslaughter and there was a protest downtown. And I was

> there with my grandmother and her sister participated and I went along. I can remember the chants of "Don't go on the mall," because at that [time] . . . downtown there was an outdoor mall. And it was paved. Traffic couldn't go down the street. It's one of the biggest mistakes they made in the urban renewal of Wilmington. I mean it destroyed downtown. But I can remember having to help drag my grandmother and aunt off of the mall because the cops on the horses were beating people in the head. These women were senior citizens taking blows to the head.

Gerald's family had very high expectations regarding education. He described his mother, in particular, as especially demanding. Yet education would become a particularly volatile issue as Gerald went through high school in the late 1970s. Indeed, large white demonstrations against newly proposed integrative busing programs were sweeping across the nation. However, Gerald's mother was an outspoken opponent of busing programs. Even though she was in the minority in the black community, she was of the mindset that the city's black high school had great teachers but was woefully lacking in resources. Although she relented and allowed Gerald to be bused out of the city to a high school in a predominantly affluent white neighborhood, Gerald recalls his mother attending many community meetings with politicians shouting in their faces, "Integrate the money."

Interviewer: Where did you go to school?

Gerald: I was at one high school until my junior year. That was the year before busing, I had no problems. You know white kids were friendly. I mean a couple kids you gave a little shit. But for the most part, I had white friends as well as black friends. The year busing started was my senior year in high school. And that's when the crap really hit the fan. Yeah, even some of the teachers went on strike, and it was really a mess. The same kids I was buddies with, because of the influence of their parents, became racist assholes, and I got suspended for fighting probably like four or five times before the end of the year. And you know the year before all this mess I had never got suspended once.

Interviewer: Wow, it was really chaotic times.

Gerald: Yeah, I could remember walking home from school and there were parents [of white kids] running up on the law shouting at us.

Interviewer: So this is happening in your senior year of high school?

Gerald: February of my senior year, I'm an honor student and I got kicked out for felonious assault. . . . I had hung out with a white kid who I'd meet in the library. I've always been a reader. So sometimes I came out of school late. And I come out and these two whites kids were beating up my friend, calling him "nigger lover," so they're beating him up for hanging out with me. And it's two against one. And I jumped in, and I don't want to sound like I was a badass or anything, but I could scrap. And I was too much for the both of them, and I beat the hell out of both of them. And of course the cops come, and the school gave me the choice of facing the charges or taking expulsion. And my mother was gonna get a lawyer and fight it and all that. And I was like, "I don't even want to deal with this," so I took the expulsion. So, I went down the next week and got my GED and signed up for the air force.

Interviewer: I assumed your mom was not that pleased!

Gerald: Not at first. When I told her I was gonna sign up for the military—initially I was looking at the navy—and she was not happy about that at all. And I could remember going to the navy recruiting office and it was a mess. Man these cats were so disorganized! They had papers all over the god damn place. So I was waiting in the hall and the recruiter from the air force comes in and he says, "Are you waiting for the guys over there? Why don't you come over her and talk to me. So I go into his office and it's neat and clean and very professional. So when I came home I told my mom "I'm going in the air force." She said "all right." She was okay with that.

Gerald's story is truly remarkable. If not for the white racial hostilities of the time, it is likely that he would never have joined the military. As an honor student he would have, indeed, almost certainly gone on to college. But the racial turmoil that engulfed his high school radically altered his life circumstances. It is all the more remarkable that he only had a few months before graduation. Given the circumstances, one might have expected in the late 1970s a more forgiving high school principal. But the racial conditions of the time literally transformed schools into places of racial strife and desperation for young black males, even those with a bright future like Gerald. While joining the air force is not, at least seemingly at this point, an altogether negative turning point in Gerald's life, the cumulative experience of having to adapt to an institution now fraught with uncertainty and a "kill or be killed" culture would prove to have lasting implications for Gerald. As we will see in the stories of other AVF era veterans of color, the backlash against the civil rights movement transformed the lives of young black men in precarious ways. Indeed, for many, the decision to enlist in the military was not simply to escape the ghetto but to fight for one's freedom. Beginning in the 1980s, the kind of "prison or the military" quandary that Gerald found himself in becomes a much higher stakes situation for many black veterans of the AVF era. However, the decision to enlist for some was not one they had any control over—indeed, they enlisted as part of an ultimatum given to them in court by a judge.

"YOU EITHER ENLIST IN THE MILITARY OR YOU'RE GONNA DO SOME TIME"

When I sat down to interview Jeffrey in one of IH's makeshift office spaces, I was again confronted with an African-American veteran plagued with a myriad of untreated health problems. In addition to diabetes, Jeffrey was infected with the Hepatitis C virus. This dangerous disease of the liver had clearly taken its toll on him. For our interview, he was fortunately able to get some relief from tremendous joint pains he suffered from by lying back in an office chair. It was clear to me that Jeffrey's health problems were very serious. Indeed, only a few weeks after our interview he was placed in long-term care at a VA medical center.

Jeffrey was the only veteran I interviewed who grew up in a military family. His father was a Vietnam veteran who served thirty years in uniform and was constantly on the move: "It seemed like we were moving all the time, but the bases seemed a lot alike—looking back they kinda blurred together—so, at least from what I remember about it, moving wasn't a huge deal." When I asked him about any racial conflicts he experienced on base, Jeffrey stated "Yeah, I mean we were called nigger down south, but it wasn't until years later that I even understood what was going on with that ignorance."

Jeffrey's most vivid early memories were of family life. Raised in a two-parent household, a sense of structure and discipline were instilled in Jeffrey, who was the baby of the family, and his six older siblings. In addition to requiring all his children to follow a strict regimen of household chores, Jeffrey's father required them to work outside of the house.

Interviewer: What kind of rules did your dad have and where did you work? On base?

Jeffrey: Yeah, I worked at the PX [Post-Exchange] bagging groceries.

Interviewer: How would your dad discipline you and your siblings?

Jeffrey: Oh, there were many days when you got the shit beat out of you. But my father was taking care of us the best way he knew how. He was a drunk but that was because of 'Nam. But he somehow kept it hidden pretty well. I mean it wasn't like he was one of these guys that left the family, left the wife with all those kids, you know? He hung around. He did what he had to do, in order to keep himself and his house in control.

Jeffrey describes strong kinship with his siblings: "I mean, my brothers and sisters and I always had each other's backs. We looked out for each other. I mean like with curfew, we knew we had to be in by midnight, and we sure as hell weren't coming in at three or four o'clock in the morning. Because my father would be waiting for you! Hell, I remember getting dragged in the house by my brothers at like 11:59 because being late just wasn't an option [laughs]."

Jeffrey's biggest struggles came in school. He describes his teachers as having low expectations in "a black boy, I guess. But then again I wasn't the best student, I wasn't stupid but school was boring and the teachers were never in my corner. But I still managed to get by without doing a lot of work."

Interviewer: How did your father react?

Jeffrey: My father always said to me, "Everything comes so easy to you," and he was probably right. I mean, I didn't have to study to pass a test. I played sports in high school and they came pretty natural. My grandmother gave me a set of drums, and I taught myself how to play. I never felt challenged growing up.

Interviewer: So what led you to the military?

Jeffrey: I started doing stupid stuff out of boredom. Experimenting with dope and got into some fights in school and what not. I got busted for shoplifting a few times, all stupid stuff. And by that time, my father had kicked me out of the house. So I actually ended up before a judge and he told me, "Son, you're eighteen now so you either enlist in the military or you're gonna do some time." I mean, I had just turned eighteen. I dropped out of high school—which was nothing 'cuz I gave up on school years ago any way—you know what I'm saying? So, anyways, I got my GED and joined the military.

Jeffrey was one of two black veterans interviewed that were given the proverbial "enlist or do time" ultimatum by a judge. Given the relative isolation of life on a military base, Jeffrey's pre-military years clearly differed from the other veterans I interviewed. On the other hand, many respondents of the AVF era described problems with parental figures. Despite being physically abused by an alcoholic father, Jeffrey even looked back at his father with reverence. Perhaps, given his father's ability to stay with the family—something that became increasingly challenging for black men of that generation to do—Jeffrey is able to rationalize his father's behavior in a more favorable light. Another possible explanation is revealed in his own experience as a father after service in the military. Jeffrey struggled in relationships and, unlike his father, did become estranged from his family.[5] Perhaps he looks up to his father's resolve to maintain a nuclear family precisely because it was a goal he was not able to achieve in his own life. As the following exchange reveals, Jeffrey's early socialization into a narrowly defined set of gender norms defined by harsh discipline and control—what he describes as what it means to be "the man of the house"—he attributes to his father:

Interviewer: With your own kids, do you think your dad had an influence on you?

Jeffrey: Oh, no doubt. No doubt. Being a father you gotta throw down the law, and show who's the man of the house.

Interviewer: Do you see your kids today?

Jeffrey: Not much, I mean my own problems with drugs and blowing up on my ex-wife. I think there's some distance there. But my son texts me once in awhile. But when I was really deep into addiction I smacked his mother and him around a lot. And then when I lost my job, I stopped paying childcare support.

Interviewer: What happened?

Jeffrey: Crack is what happened! Heroin is was happened too. When I got out of the service my family was up in Jersey. And I couldn't hold down any jobs. It was so god damn frustrating. I drove trucks in the military, so you'd think I could get a job with all my experience. I can operate forklifts too. But there was no steady work, so one thing led to another and I started using. I mean, at that time it was all over the city. But so

> were the police. So, I actually got locked up for that—I bought a rock from some undercover cop who nailed me—and I did my first bid. And jail ain't shit for anything; people be using in there and everything else. So things were not good for a long while. And by the time I got myself to the VA for treatment and what not, I lost touch with my son. . . . So I'm not too sure what's going on in his life. Plus, I got too much now going on that I gotta deal with my own life and problems.

The nexus between chronic unemployment and drug abuse is well documented in the literature. However, it is rarely contextualized in the particulars of an unfolding series of lived events. Jeffrey's story speaks to the devastating impact of the urban drug war in the lives of African-American men. As a scorned veteran—indeed, as someone who acquired skills in the military only to return home to a volatile and unforgiving job market—so began his downward spiral into serious drug abuse, incarceration, and the severing of his own role as a father. Rather than a single turning point, there is a confluence of life-changing events that illuminate Jeffrey's downward spiral.

"BE ALL YOU CAN BE"

When I first met Martin (age 44) at IH, I was surprised by how young he looked. He may have been forty-four but he could have easily passed for twenty-two. He had boyish good looks with very round eyes and a voice barely above a whisper. But what appeared as a vision of youth on the outside was much more problematic on the inside. Specifically, Martin suffered from many serious ailments, including chronic asthma and heart disease. Indeed, I would learn later from him that his quiet voice was the product of these conditions, which left him profoundly weakened.

In contrast to Jeffrey's upbringing in a two-parent family on a military base, Martin's parents were divorced when he was very young. Both he and his sister were raised by their mother. However, tragedy struck just at age 16 when his mother suddenly passed away. Martin made it clear that talking about the circumstances surrounding the loss of his mother was not "somewhere I want to go." So I moved gingerly to a next question about the aftermath of his mother's death:

Interviewer: I'm so sorry. . . . So what happened after you lost your mother?

Martin: It really hit me hard that I had nowhere to go. I went to live with my father, but he didn't want me there. So, I went to live with my aunt, then another aunt and another aunt. I mean it got to the point where I wanted to stop moving. I wanted to stop going from place to place and wanted to stop depending on people.

Somehow in spite of his tremendously unstable living situation, Martin was able to stay with one aunt long enough to finish high school. After high school, a major turning point for Martin was joining the U.S. Job Corps where he learned to be an electrician. Martin took full advantage of this opportunity and also learned glazing (e.g., putting glass into high-rise buildings and office buildings) and became a certified commercial painter. It was also at this time that Martin joined the Army Reserves.

Interviewer: So why did you enlist?

Martin: I actually joined the Army Reserves because, for me, it was like "be all you can be." That was the ticket. That was the slogan, and I thought it was pretty good.

Interviewer: Was your aunt happy for you?

Martin: No, she never knew because after I got my high school degree she moved again and I was on my own. I was kicked out of every place I stayed. I mean, you gotta understand my family; they're not at all supportive. They just wanted me to help with rent—I mean they was living in the 'hood—so when I wanted to make a change, I never looked back, and to this day I have had very little contact with any of my family and just have a few friends.

Interviewer: So you just kept at it, no matter the situation.

Martin: Yeah, pretty much. I had to adapt and be self-sufficient and not live with people whose lifestyle that wasn't mine. After staying with them and how I was treated, I don't even really consider them my family. I've never had any family. I mean, after my mom died I moved in with my dad who I had barely seen in years. And then like two months later, he put my all of my things in garbage bags on the sidewalk one night.

Interviewer: Why do you think he did that?

Martin: I think he wanted me to drop out of high school and get a job to help pay the rent. I mean he was scum. He could never hold down a job. He's a drunk and always broke. But just throwing everything I owned on the sidewalk? I mean,

> damn, that was real cold. So Job Corps and the military were for me, it was my opportunity to get away from all that negative stuff.

Martin's pre-military experience provides a strong contrast to Jeffrey. For Martin, his father was anything but supportive. He is absolutely unapologetic about what he perceives as the utter betrayal of his family members, and his father's actions represent to him the worst of an already tumultuous living situation. The turning point that sets in motion this difficult set of circumstances is not run-ins with the criminal justice system or problems in school, but the death of his mother when Martin was only 16 years of age. Remarkably, Martin perseveres in the face of tremendous adversity and graduates high school, joins the U.S. Jobs Corps, and the Army Reserves.

"HE'S TALKING A THREE-YEAR, STEADY JOB"

When Gregory (age 47) met me outside at one of IH's picnic tables, he was five minutes late as he had just returned from the VA medical center. Gregory had a badly infected foot caused by a nail he had stepped on approximately a month earlier. He tried to, in his words, "suck it up," but the pain became unbearable, as well as the stench of a fungal infection that had developed. Fortunately, Gregory was well enough to participate in an interview.

When I asked about his youth, he focused on high school. Specifically, a major turning point for Gregory was his high-school girlfriend's pregnancy. Indeed, it was the major catalyst for his decision to enlist in the military.

Interviewer: So tell me about the area thirty years ago.

Gregory: You know, it was not exactly the best family environment and still ain't; if anything it's gotten worse. This city is so small and you got the jail right down the block. There was a lot bad elements, drugs and shootings and what have you. But I was lucky to go to a decent high school away from here. I was a pretty good student. But then my girlfriend got pregnant.

Interviewer: Okay, so what happens next?

Gregory: I almost pissed myself [laughs]. But we both managed somehow to graduate from high school. . . . But my father, who was a Vietnam vet and a hard ass told me I had to get a job. Basically he was like: "You got her pregnant, you gotta take care of her, so you need to get you a job." But all of the jobs that I went for were temporary. There wasn't a single

> job I could find that were guaranteed steady work. You know, they call you in to do construction and if it rains, so you don't work. You know, if the weather is cold, you don't work. I mean little odd jobs here and there, they weren't making no money. They weren't paying nothing.

Under tremendous pressure from both his father and his girlfriend's family, Gregory came to the conclusion that he had run out of options. His father had always expressed a deep pride in military service, so Gregory turned back to him for advice:

> My pops told me about what the military had to offer and, at the time, my cousin was trying to enlist but he kept failing the ASVAB [Army entrance exam]. My cousin lived in the 'hood too, right around the corner from us, and I always got better grades than him, so I'm like, "How hard can it be?" And I went to the recruiter, and he told me about how if you put in three years, the government will guarantee you pay for the time you do there. So he's talking a three-year steady job. I'm like hmm. . . . I can definitely take care of a child and girlfriend that way. So I took the exam and scored real high.

After a week of thinking it over with his family, Gregory decided to formally enlist. In addition to the military as a way to attend to his responsibilities as a young and impoverished father, Gregory also explains that the chance to travel made the military a big draw for him: "I mean I haven't ever been nowhere and I ain't gonna get nowhere working these little jobs. And you're talking about guaranteed pay. So I said, "Hey, I'll give it a try," so I went in.

While the circumstances surrounding Gregory's story aren't unusual, the constant struggle to find gainful employment reveals how enlisting in the military was a calculation based almost purely in terms of economic survival. In contrast to Jeffrey, he describes himself as a good student and his father as a "hard ass" but also someone he felt comfortable turning to for advice. While he never discussed his father in more detail, Gregory neither reveres him nor holds the kind of contempt that Martin has for a father he described as "scum." Echoing many of the "freedom from the 'hood" sentiments of the other respondents, Jeffrey is one of the only veterans I interviewed who described the draw of the military's guaranteed pay. This is likely less a function of Gregory's erroneous belief that the pay would be good, but due more to his circumstances as a new father desperate to find a steady means of financial support for his girlfriend and newborn child.

"EITHER IT WAS THAT OR THE STREETS"

"Do you want to see where I grew up?" I nodded, and Terrence (age 51) and I hopped into my car and drove a few blocks from IH. "There it is. Can you see the construction going on?" I nodded, looking at a presently empty lot with a crane and numerous bulldozers. "Well, that's where our project used to be. It has since been knocked down and they're going to rebuild it with new Section 8 houses." Terrence seemed very anxious from the outset of our interview. After asking him a few background questions about his health, he told me that he suffered from panic disorder as well as PTSD. Like the others I interviewed at IH, it was pretty obvious he was not sleeping well either. Terrence explained his present situation:

Interviewer: How has it been for you here so far?

Terrence: Okay, except for my roommate. I need sleep. I mean I sleep late all the time. But he's loud and fussing with the TV. It's pretty cramped in there too, so it's hard. He also has eaten some of my food without asking, so it ain't going well. But I just make do with it. I'll try to get in another room, but I know it's pretty crowded here right now. But it's better than the last place I was in.

Interviewer: Where was that?

Terrence: Anywhere! I was living on the streets on benches and staying on my cousin's couch whenever I could. But, yeah, I was nowhere for a year before I come here.

When I asked Terrence about growing up in the projects, he began by describing how he and his six siblings spent most of their time. Specifically, he described a city park on the edge of a predominantly white, working-class suburb and the city.

Interviewer: Tell me about the park.

Terrence: Yeah, this city so small, so it was right down the street from us. Real, real nice then. Basketball courts and trees and paths to run around and what not. So my brothers and sisters and I always went there. But we also found out pretty quickly that it was dangerous.

Interviewer: How so?

Terrence: That's where we had our first experience with the teenage Ku Klux Klan groups—they wore jean jackets with KKK patches—and I learned that this is where they had drawn

> their line. They went into the park to keep the blacks from the city from coming in there. They wouldn't always be there, but my brothers, sister, and I got chased outta there many times. They would be yelling "Go home niggers! This isn't your park!" Blah, blah, blah. . . . It was ignorant BS. But we kept coming back anyway [laughs]!

Like other veterans of his generation, Terrence describes a racially volatile climate in Wilmington. The youth Klan group was likely part of a resurgent white racist backlash against integration efforts. Indeed, the fight by whites to block integration and reinforce black exclusion not only involved schools but also other public spaces outside ghettoized neighborhoods, including public parks. In contrast to Gerald's supportive black nationalist mother, grandmother, and aunt, Terrence's home life was chaotic from an early age. He grew up in a family of eight in a small apartment in an impoverished section of the neighborhood. Although he lived with two parents, Terrence describes his abusive and controlling stepfather as "tearing our family apart."

Interviewer: Tell me about what happened with your stepdad.

Terrence: Well, all six of us rebelled. We ran away from home. We slept in alleyways, wherever, but typically only a few days would go by and we'd get picked up by the cops.

Eventually Terrence and his siblings were put into foster care. In contrast to Vietnam era veteran Charles, Terrence described his experience in foster care as very negative:

> I fought against being taken away from my momma every chance I could get. I blame my stepdad for everything. We were young kids and we needed our momma. I mean, my dad worked nights and so she was the one who raised us. But any time we saw [stepdad's name] he was yelling or beating up on us and my mom. Without her, the state split us up and so we were in foster care basically alone. It took a heavy toll on me growing up. . . . I mean, I was a decent student, but I started making bad grades because I stopped caring. Looking back, I was definitely having some problems with depression but back then it wasn't discovered and no one talked about it. . . . But I finally got scared of what was happening to me, especially when I got a report card with all failing grades. I would never have gotten a report card like that if I had stayed with my mother. My mother had us disciplined to the point to where she knew we were capable of making good grades.

After bouncing from foster homes, Terrence continued to struggle academically in high school.

Interviewer: How did the constant moving impact your school work?

Terrence: I almost flunked the eleventh grade. But then I switched to a technical school and got excellent training in plumbing. But I was stupid and got kicked out of that program for pulling a fire alarm. It was just stupidity. So, I ended up in a group home. We would do all of our school work there and that's where I eventually graduated from high school.

When I asked Terrence about his decision to enlist in the military his explanation was sobering and somewhat similar to Martin's experience. However, Terrence described the situation not as a kind of liberation from difficult family life, but a decision made out of desperation:

Interviewer: So what led you to enlist?

Terrence: I had no place to go after I graduated. It was the only option I had. Either it was that or the streets. I didn't know what else to do. And that's why I went to talk to a recruiter for the Navy, but I failed the test. He told me I didn't score high enough. I was really upset about that. But I took those same scores over to the army recruiter, and that's when they told me that I scored very low but I qualified for a combat MOS and it was field artillery. I didn't have no problem with that. I always felt that a combat MOS was the place to be anyway. And I had no problem serving my country. I mean, I have a lot of pride in being the kind of veteran who was in field artillery. I just feel that field artillery was the backbone of the infantry. When things get really rough, and they see something coming, they called us up, and we were the ones that actually started doing stuff [laughs].

Terrence's pathway to the military is anything but linear. He grew up in poverty and was subjected to a broader climate of racism from an early age. Terrence's story of his family life is simultaneously one of abandonment and feelings of great attachment to his mother. Indeed, Terrence describes his mother's strict and structured approach to schoolwork, it is a story of the possibilities of upward educational mobility slipping away. Terrence is left on his own to bounce from foster home to foster home, from one failed school experience to another. While his description of his decision to enlist is one of sheer desperation—indeed, in the next chapter unsurprisingly Terrence's experience in the military is extraordinarily tumultuous—one easily overlooks how accomplishments he mentions (e.g., receiving training as a plumber at a technical school) will create a new set of possibilities in his life. I'll explore this remarkable turn of events in the book's conclusion.

"I WAS CARRYING ON A FAMILY TRADITION"

Forty-five-year-old Vincent had a turbulent childhood. He was born very prematurely. The physician who delivered him explained to his parents that it was very likely that he would suffer from a mental disability. However, from the earliest age Vincent remembers his parents as thoroughly committed to "providing me with a normal childhood. And my dad, especially, was very strict about education."

Interviewer: Tell me about that, how did your folks approach your education?

Vincent: When I entered into first grade, I was reading at a third grade level. I mean my parents were not playing around. I think my dad's experience in the military—he was a Vietnam vet—had a lot to do with it. I mean, we had to put our books in a proper place every time. And a lot of time I'd want to get up and watch TV and he said, "No, you gotta sit down and focus." My dad wanted us to go to college.

Interviewer: Did your dad use the GI Bill and get a college degree?

Vincent: He had big dreams for us. I mean he'd tell us stories and show us pictures of poverty stricken countries, and tell us how thankful we should be and not to throw away the opportunities given to us. He wanted to see one of his kids get a college degree, without question. It was like his mission in life. . . . He was tough, but I looked up to him so much. . . . Man, I tear up thinking about when he died. . . . But we can talk about that later if you wanna.

Interviewer: Definitely. I mean as much as you're able to talk about.

Like many generations of African Americans before him, Vincent's family placed a premium on education. And Vince had tremendous respect for his father and looked up to him as a hero figure. However, a major turning point for his entire family came after the tragic death of his youngest brother who was struck and killed by an automobile at the age of 4.

Interviewer: Oh. . . . I'm so sorry about your brother. . . . That must have been devastating.

Vincent: More than my family could handle. I mean it was crazy. I look back now and, you know, it was me who should have died. It's a miracle that I was alive! And my dad worked himself to the bone—you talk about strong man. He had these big, calloused hands and was strong like a bear from

	hauling slabs of concrete around all those years. But once Sam, my baby brother, died, it was like everything in our family died with him.
Interviewer:	Do you mind talking a little about that?
Vincent:	I mean, we were literally in shock for weeks. And my father always drank—I think it was his way of dealing with the memories of fighting in the war, too—but he really started drinking heavily after Sam was killed. And then he would just disappear for days on end. To this day, I'm not really sure where he would go, but that took a huge toll on me and my sister and mom. And my parents eventually separated. It was something I didn't understand at the time—I mean they loved each other and us kids more than life itself—but looking back it was just too much to handle.
Interviewer:	Tell me about your parents' separation.
Vincent:	My parents dealt with it the best they could, but once my dad left I noticed the discipline left with him. So my mom raised us, but we still got to see him a lot and we also stayed with my grandparents. And my dad seemed to sober up more and stayed available to me. I remember really wanting to move in with him. But my dad knew it was best for my mom to raise us.

In high school, Vincent began to struggle academically. Similar to Gerald and Terrence, Vincent was caught in the white racist backlash of the times. Like Gerald, the backlash against school busing took an enormous toll on him. Compounded by his parents' separation and loss of his younger brother, Vincent began to act out. He describes the opportunity to go to a good school as a "set-up." There he got into many fights in school and felt especially alienated by his teachers.

Interviewer:	What happened with school?
Vincent:	One of the biggest let-downs was high school. I mean all of the sudden we're getting a chance to go to the prissy white school in the suburbs. But like my dad, I saw it as an opportunity. But, man, I'm telling you it felt like a set-up. From day one, I remember them putting us in the special classes. I remember feeling like they was doing me a favor letting me be there. I mean I was pretty chill before bussing, but now it was all about race and standing your ground. We were feared simply because we were black. And the tough

guy white racists would get their asses beat by us. But it was stupid. We were there to learn, not to fight. I'm telling you it was a set-up.

Although Vincent did not experience the kind of volatile race riots that resulted in a major turning point in Gerald's life, he described developing feelings of deep alienation:

Interviewer: Were there any full on race riots?

Vincent: Not that extreme. But it damned sure felt like I spent more time suspended than in class. Just fighting all the time. It probably would have been better if I was home schooled. Just like my mom and pops did with us when we were young, only full time. This was no way to learn in that kind of environment where people wanted to see you fail. I mean my teachers at our high school pretty much gave up on me, and so I gave up on them. You know, I was just a thug in their eyes. And they were probably right. I was fighting all the time and just caught up showing the whites that we blacks were no one's chump, you know what I'm saying? It was just putting on a front.

Vincent provides profound insight into what it meant to live through this racially tumultuous period. At the institutional level, Vincent was no longer a student but a thug. One can also see how the failure to address the seriousness of the situation by white political and educational elites transformed the school into a kind of prison and his teachers into captors. Despite his downward spiral educationally, Vincent's parents' continued to support him. Indeed, even after he decided to drop out of high school and had what he described as "numerous run-ins with the police," Vincent describes his parents' support as unrelenting.

Interviewer: How did your parents react to when you dropped out?

Vincent: They was always there for me. Even, my dad. He'd show up in court when I was going before judges. When I had to meet with the principal about some mess. Whatever it was, he was behind me. And you know what? My parents never demeaned me. I mean they were disappointed, but their love was unconditional.

Just like Jeffrey's entryway into the military, Vincent also faced a judge's ultimatum. However, in contrast to Jeffrey's father who, by that time, had kicked him out of the house, Vincent describes his parents as continuing to support him:

Interviewer: Tell me about how you ended up in the marines.

Vincent: Ha! Yup, it was going up before a judge. He had enough of seeing my face. This black judge. . . . I can't remember his last name. . . . But he said, "Your choice, military or get locked up."

Interviewer: How did having to make that decision make you feel?

Vincent: I actually was shocked, because I thought I was going away this time. I mean, a lot of young blacks were getting locked up, so I thought it was my time. So I was excited about the opportunity. I knew I was heading down the wrong path, so the service probably saved my life. And my father was really proud. He told me right there in the courthouse that I was carrying on a family tradition and hugged me. So I felt good.

The turn of events in Vincent's life began with the death of his youngest brother and the subsequent dissolution of his parents' marriage. At the same time, the volatile historical circumstances are critical for understanding subsequent events. Despite the great hope of school integration, Vincent felt the oppression of the white educational system's low expectations for young black males. Like Gerald, Vincent describes fighting as perhaps the singular way for him to save face as a racialized outsider. But this experience profoundly stigmatized him in the eyes of his teachers. Distressingly, the so-called thug label that he was branded with became a self-fulfilling prophecy. Vincent began a precipitous downward trajectory into petty crime and eventually dropped out of high school altogether. Yet despite it all, his family stood by him. Even when faced by a judge's final ultimatum, his decision to join the military was met with not his father's derision but support. Indeed, Vincent describes his father as transforming a moment that otherwise would be profoundly tumultuous in the lives of most young men, into a time of great pride about his son's future in the military.

"I TOOK WHAT SHE SAID ABOUT THE MILITARY AS A CHALLENGE"

Stephen (age 32) was one of the younger veterans I interviewed. However, he had been through a lot of challenging circumstances in his life, including service in the Marine Corps during a bloody conflagration between warring tribes in East Timor, Indonesia. Stephen grew up in one of Wilmington's newer housing projects; however, the neighborhood was a prime target for undercover buy-bust operations by the police. As a child of America's ongoing drug war, Stephen recalls many of his neighbors "being locked up in droves for possession." But from an early age his parents were able to keep him focused on school. Like other AVF era respondents, Stephen's father served in Vietnam. Stephen recalls his father being a strict disciplinarian. However, after his parents divorced when he was 5 years old, he had little contact with his dad. In contrast to other veterans who maintained relationships with their fathers, the next time Stephen would see his dad was at the age of 16 shortly before be he succumbed to a long battle with cancer. Stephen's mother remarried but he describes his stepdad "as never really a father figure to me." Stephen and his siblings viewed their stepfather first and foremost, in Stephen's words, as "a financial provider."

In a tragic twist of fate, however, Stephen's stepfather was not with his family very long. Under circumstances that were never entirely made clear to him, his stepfather apparently fatally shot himself in front of the family. Although, Stephen didn't want to talk about this profoundly traumatizing event in more detail, he did disclose that he never sought any counseling and "just kept it buried it inside."[6] After learning about these especially traumatic events, we turned to his youth:

Stephen: In my neighborhood, I got beat up a lot growing up, because I think everyone knew I didn't have an older brother to get my back. I got picked on. There were all these cliques, and I was the outcast. But I didn't want to get in trouble. I wasn't a gangster. So I did a lot of running growing up and I had a bike [laughs]. I mean, I rode my bike all over the city.

Unlike most other respondents, Stephen avoided violent confrontation during his childhood at all costs. Feeling outnumbered and fearing the consequences of retaliation, he kept a low profile both by ignoring taunting peers and quite literally running away from conflict. Moreover, Stephen describes his strict religious upbringing as playing a major role in developing this discipline:

> There was always a voice inside of me that gangbanging was the wrong thing to do. And between my mom, my grandmother, and uncle, they used to make me read scripture. I spent most of my summers with my grandmother, and we prayed in the morning and before I went to bed at night. It was challenging growing up, but I believe it was very helpful.

Stephen's biggest challenges came as a young black man in a high school that had very high drop-out rates. School discipline was also very strict, but Stephen was a diligent student and never faced any challenges until his junior year.

Interviewer: You mentioned your junior year of high school as challenging, can you tell me what happened?

Stephen: My guidance counselor told me that my mom didn't have the money to send me to college, I didn't have the grades to get an academic scholarship, and she didn't think I was cut out for the military. So she said, "I really don't know what you're going to do with your life." And I said, "You actually get paid to tell kids this stuff [laughs]?" So it was kind of cool to go back to my school and have my guidance counselor see me in my Marine Corps uniform. I mean, I took what she said about the military as a challenge.

Stephen saw his enlistment decision as a very straightforward calculus: "I could stay here in Delaware with no money for college, try to get a job, or I can go travel and see the world!? I mean it's a no-brainer. Plus, I didn't see any other possible way that I could get the money for college. And the Marine Corps had the best uniforms! So there was no way I was going to pass all of this up." Since he was a self-described "momma's boy," Stephen's mother was clearly concerned by her son's decision to enlist: "She understood, but didn't want me in harm's way. But she told me that no matter what decision I made, she would support me."

Stephen's early childhood was characterized by the loss of his birth father at an early age and the thoroughly traumatizing experience of having to witness his stepfather's suicide. At the same time, he describes being able to protect himself from the dangers of street life. Stephen's story, indeed, illuminates the vital role of religious faith in his life. Even in the absence of a steady father figure and a disturbing family tragedy, Stephen was able to persevere. As will be seen, the church plays an essential role for understanding how some African-American veterans, especially after they leave the military, can be resilient even in the face of extremely dire circumstances (see chapter 5). However, Stephen, even at an early age, describes his faith as providing him with the strength to remain non-violent. One might have thought that this dogged commitment would carry over into stellar academic achievement. However, as a mediocre student he turns to a school guidance counselor who provides only negative feedback. Rather than responding negatively to a callous high school guidance counselor's bleak evaluation of his future, Stephen becomes even more determined to become a Marine.

"I FELT LIKE AFTER 9/11 THAT I COULD BE PART OF HISTORY"

Seeking more interviews with African-American veterans of the Iraq war, I interviewed Andre (age 28) over the telephone. Like all the respondents I interviewed, Andre's pre-military life provides important insights of a unique turning point in the AVF era. During Operation Iraqi Freedom, far more soldiers participated in dangerous combat operations at any time since the Vietnam War. Although, a major theme that emerged in Andre's story was struggle, his early childhood is a more nuanced tale of resilience and finding meaning in one's life after high school. Although Andre did not serve with Trey (see chapter 2), their stories are remarkably similar. Andre also received a negative discharge from the marines under very similar circumstances as Trey. While his understandably troubled outlook was palpable—after all, it had only been a very short time since he received a bad conduct discharge—Andre was very willing to be interviewed.

Interviewer: So tell me about your upbringing. . . . Where did you grow up?

Andre: I was born in Montgomery, Alabama, but in the first grade, our family moved to California for a little less than a year.

Interviewer: What was that like going from the South to the West Coast?

Andre: It was like night and day and eye opening for me, especially at such a young age. I did most of first grade in California and there my grades were excellent.

Interviewer: What was the school like?

Andre: The school was real diverse racially. I mean black kids all sat together at lunch or whatever—but we were all friends with the white kids and the Hispanic kids—both inside and outside of school. I mean race meant nothing out there. Everybody's cool with everybody, color didn't seem to matter. It wasn't until we moved back to Alabama—which was real confusing to me because we hadn't even lived in California for ten months—that I started running into racism. What I'm trying to say is this: I was only in the first grade, but when I got back down in Alabama, I knew that in the 1980s it still meant you were seen as inferior if you were black.

Interviewer: Really, even in the 1980s? Tell me about that experience.

Andre: You see, when I moved back to Alabama, the schools were so racist. Even though the work was very easy for me, I went from being recognized as an outstanding student in the first half of first grade in California to being recognized as not only a bad student but, by the end of first grade, my homeroom teacher actually recommended to my mother that I should be held back a year and put me in special education.

Andre believes his attempt to talk with white kids in his Alabama school—what he perceived to be an act of defiance against the school's rigid color-line—triggered his white homeroom teacher to retaliate against him. Indeed, Andre described the entire school as pervasively operating according to this de facto policy:

> I mean, what my homeroom teacher was trying to do—telling me who my friends were gonna be, telling me I couldn't talk to white kids—was happening to all black kids down there. I mean, she literally told me, "You see the little black kids with the nappy hair and dirty noses? Well those are gonna be your only friends." And it went on like this until the seventh grade. Thankfully, my mother would battle my homeroom teacher and the school, otherwise I would have been sent to an alternative school like many of the other black kids in the school. I mean, it was crazy! I only had homeroom for fifteen minutes a day each morning, and this woman tried to send me to alternative school three times.

Fortunately for Andre, high school was a much more positive experience. Even though he long struggled with a childhood foot injury that left him with agonizing bone spurs and thus limited his athletic activities throughout most of his childhood, Andre was obsessed with sports and played two years of varsity football.

Interviewer: It sounds like high school down there was a much more positive experience for you?

Andre: I had a lot of pride in my high school and it was a lot of fun. The white principals weren't racist. . . . There weren't any fights; it was really a safe environment, and if you were doing something like ROTC or football, then the team effort makes racism even less of an issue. You know what I'm saying? Like on the football team all of us are brothers no matter what color you are. That kind of opened us up. It opened me up not to be racist. I mean my homeboy was white—one of my closest friends in high school—I could go over to his house at three o'clock in the morning and get a soda if I wanted to. And the military, up until Iraq, was the same way for me.

Andre's decision to enlist in the military began in his senior year of high school. He joined the Marine Corps' DET. However, soon after the events of September 11, 2001, it became clear to him that he wanted to go to Iraq.

Interviewer: Tell me about your decision to enlist.

Andre: I wanted to be the best. I wanted to be looked at as honorable. I mean my cousins were active duty in the army at the time, but I really did not pay them any attention whatsoever. I mean, I knew I wanted to do something *extra* ordinary. Ever since I was a kid I wanted go to the NFL, be an astronaut, or be a pilot. But two of those dreams were killed, because I'm six foot two, so I'm too tall to be an astronaut. And I'm too tall to be a pilot, so because of my foot—I mean, it got better and all, but I never excelled enough to play in the NFL or even college ball—so that wasn't going to happen. But I stayed focused. I thought hard about what the most honorable thing I can do was, so I decided I'll be a Marine.

Interviewer: Tell me about your final decision.

Andre: In addition to what I told you [see quote from the beginning of this chapter], I felt this war really could be a positive step toward transcending the racial boundary in our country. I thought that with more black people being veterans and going over there and doing something that should be looked at differently when we come home. . . I felt like after 9/11 that I could be part of history. I wanted to be a part of that.

Andre's story of "proving oneself" is similar to Stephen's response to his high school guidance counselor. Although Andre didn't experience the kind of viscerally traumatic events that befell Stephen in his youth, Andre's constant battle to prove himself in elementary school seemed to be an important turning point in his life. The constant racial animus of a homeroom teacher—indeed, a teacher who wanted him to be transferred to a school for students with learning disabilities—was never something Andre describes as even remotely accepting. Importantly, his mother stood up to school officials on his behalf. Despite facing such extreme institutional adversity at a young age, it seems likely that this experience left Andre with an even greater sense of resolve and self-efficacy. Indeed, Andre described his struggle with a serious debilitating foot injury as just another challenge to overcome in high school. Perhaps more importantly was the strong educational capital Andre accumulated in high school. In contrast to elementary school, he describes his high school experience in glowing terms similar to Vietnam era veteran Mel. Indeed, the courage to "dream big" that Mel described was a major part of Andre's last year of high school. For Andre, joining the marines soon after the momentous events of September 11, 2001, was both a chance to do something "*extra* ordinary" but also as an opportunity to be a part of a history he believed might be characterized by stronger racial unity.

CONCLUSION

The pre-military life stories of Vietnam and AVF era African-American veterans illuminate the power of a life history approach. First, it is clear how important *social capital* and *social networks* are for both generations of veterans. Parents, extended family members, friends, and teachers all shaped decisions to join up. At the same time, for some respondents it was profound *social deficits* that created a distinct lack of positive connections. For Vincent the hostile racial climate of the time led him to confront the "prison or military" ultimatum that is so often trivialized in popular culture. Far from trivial, this situation emerges in the context of broader institutional failures of the school. Vincent comes to this decision in the context of a series of traumatizing events, including the death of his younger brother, the divorce of parents he described as both nurturing and supportive, and the aforementioned racial stigma associated with being a black student bused to a white school that saw him as an outcast.

The broader racial conditions of the time were also critical for understanding the experiences of Vietnam era vets. The grievous conditions of Jim Crow segregation and extreme racial isolation serves as perhaps the clearest example. The interconnected traumas of hyper-surveillance, forced segregation, and racial isolation serve as a critical backdrop for understanding the particulars of African-American veterans' lives. Beyond being forced to live in the well documented separatist conditions of black and white living spaces and institutions, black Vietnam Era veterans and their family members are, in effect, forced to make it on their own. This is not to downplay the challenging experiences of white veterans that are well-documented in the typically color-blind histories of Vietnam. However, it is clear that forced racial isolation and, as Earl described, a dominant culture that makes it clear that "you are not welcome on this earth as a black person" provide a window into a uniquely brutal set of racialized conditions.

AVF era veterans describe conditions of marginality that are less overtly racist than their Vietnam era counterparts. However, continued de facto racial segregation combined especially with racially hostile school environments and the well-documented racially targeted drug war (see especially chapter 4) illuminate the uniquely *racial* pains confronted by African-American veterans of a more recent generation. In the absence of conscription, moreover, AVF era veterans such as Terrence describe his decision to join the military as driven by sheer survival. Finally, African-American veterans of both eras describe their decisions to join up as influenced by family members, especially fathers who served in previous eras. In chapter five, it will become clearer how some such veterans have to negotiate traumatic situations that may be exasperated by their veteran fathers who may abuse alcohol and subject family members to a violently intimate war at home. In the next chapter, I turn to the next phase of these men's lives: Their experiences in the service.

Chapter Four

In the Service

Mel: Well, after the fight we got called down into the lieutenant's tent. And the white guy went in first and was in there for about a minute. Then I got in there and he looks at me and says, "Let me tell you what, I don't like no niggers in my Marine Corps." And I said, "Okay then, I guarantee that you will be dead tomorrow," and I walked right out. And I went down and told the guys in my squad, and they were like let's get him now. And I was like, "No, no let's wait." We'll give him a chance to get off of this mountain. And he was gone. He wasn't on there the next day. . . . I mean, we were in combat and we didn't have time for that kind of BS.

Gerald: I honestly believe it was my background. I was smart, a good shot, but they had come to see me as a thug. Someone who could kill without conscience. It was absolutely fucked up. They had no business doing this to me, but it's exactly what they did. In their eyes I was just another nigger.

Andre: The most blatant racist thing to me was all black guys being ordered to actually go look for mines. I mean if we find one we're dead: So we never found any! [laughs]

Once African-American veterans enter into the military, a number of important issues arise concerning training, their institutional roles, and combat experiences. While it is important to compare Vietnam and AVF veterans, the importance of within-group variation becomes clear. In considering Vietnam era veterans, when and to what extent their service experience intersects with broader conditions of racial upheaval and marginality illustrates how both experiences in the service and momentous decisions (e.g., the decision to go AWOL) may be understood. One clear and perhaps unsurprising finding, especially given the historical moment, is the experience of individual racism in the service is much more likely to be part of African-American Vietnam era veterans' experiences in the service. In contrast, AVF veterans mention racism as much more pervasive. The major exceptions are the two young Iraq veterans, Trey and Andre. Andre in particular is adamant that his negative discharge was driven by racist white military elites he describes as "hiding behind their procedures."

THE SERVICE EXPERIENCES OF VIETNAM ERA VETERANS: "WHAT THE HELL AM I DOING HERE?"

After training, Carl became a member of an armored tank crew. His first two years in the army were in Germany. Carl describes this time in very favorable terms. In fact, after Germany, Carl believed that he would be career military. However, his experience changed dramatically once his orders were cut for Vietnam. Carl served in the mechanized infantry in extraordinarily perilous conditions. In describing his experience in combat, Carl paints a visceral picture of how thoroughly dehumanizing the combat experience was for him.

Interviewer: How would a tank battle unfold over there?

Carl: We would attack in the hills, you wouldn't see a lot of VC in the open. I mean they were so dug in that we had to rely heavily on air power. I mean we would literally back off and stay a distance, and they would napalm the entire area around us. I remember the first time I saw a gunship. I gotta be honest, I wanted to kiss it [laughter], I really did fall in love with them because they took the pressure off of us. In addition to napalm, they would come in with their high technology rockets and shells. I mean, I couldn't believe it, the kind of firepower we had.

Despite Carl's awe of U.S. might, the nerve wracking experience of having to sit and wait for the enemy took a heavy toll on him. Indeed, the monotony became so bad that he temporarily deserted his unit.

Interviewer: How did that happen? Would you just take off in your tank?

Carl: No, mostly on foot. We would just run into the bush and take off and disappear. Man, we needed to blow off steam. So it got to the point where one time me and another guy in my crew were gone more than a day and we almost got

	killed by one of our own helicopters. But we cared about coming back, because we knew we were going to be in serious trouble. I mean we found a place to relax in a village, and we stayed too long.
Interviewer:	What would happen when you got back?
Carl:	We got busted. I mean, this jack ass lieutenant was ready to court-martial us. He was like, "You're going to be locked up for this." But all I got was a reprimand.

The above exchange begs two questions about Carl's subsequent experience in Vietnam: Did the reprimands have a deterrent effect on his future conduct? And how was Carl's overall attitude toward the war impacted by the reprimand?

Interviewer:	Tell me about what you were going through at the time. I mean, Germany seemed like such a positive experience, but the Vietnam War was a whole different experience.
Carl:	Yeah, it's a shame. Because if I had stayed in Germany I probably would never have left the military. Vietnam destroyed everything for me. I simply had enough of being over there. I couldn't make sense out of it.
Interviewer:	Can you explain?
Carl:	I'm gonna be honest with you: it came to the point where I literally was asking myself, "What the hell am I doing here?" I mean it was chaos and it literally came to that: "Get me the hell out of here."

When describing whether or not there was any racial conflict between white and black soldiers, Carl described a horrifying story involving the death of a white platoon sergeant he considered a "father figure." While it's tempting to link this to his own biography as the son of a single mother who never met his father, it is simply unclear if his reaction to a qualitatively gruesome situation would be different irrespective of his upbringing. Carl begins by describing his experience as a driver for a "crazy" white lieutenant he blames for the platoon sergeant's death.

Interviewer:	Was there any racial tension with you and your superiors or between soldiers?
Carl:	My platoon sergeant was white and like a father to me. He was killed because of a crazy lieutenant. And I mean the platoon sergeant really was as close to a father that I've ever had. This man was confident and trustworthy. My

lieutenant was the exact opposite. He was a threat to himself and anybody he was in contact with. I don't know where it happened—I can't even remember his name—but these were the most troubling experiences of the war and my life ever since.

Interviewer: If you don't mind, can you tell me any more details?

Carl: We were always warned that this lieutenant should be avoided like the plague. But many blacks were stuck doing a lot of driving and extra-dangerous things for white officers. So, I was ordered to be his driver and we were always on the lookout for mines. They were very big and death was almost certain for the drivers. I mean, it was very likely that I would be killed. And he had me pulling out from the column, which you were supposed to stay in, and he'd draw attention to us. But one day he ordered my platoon sergeant's vehicle out of the column, and a mine blew the vehicle and everyone in it to bits. I was totally devastated but still had to do my job, but now I would question anything the lieutenant said to me from then on. And one day he pulled his gun on me and threatened to kill me. Looking back I should have killed him, and I would have saved lives. But I just can't talk any more about it. I kinda had to force him out of my head, because he always had me in jeopardy. . . . That year in Vietnam changed my life forever.

Approximately two months later, I conducted a second interview with Carl. Here, he shared some additional details about how his career in the military came to an end.

Interviewer: So you finished your tour and came home?

Carl: Not exactly. One of the mines caught up with us. But I was real lucky—I only get sprayed with shrapnel—but it cut me up bad. They took me to a hospital. And the rest is history. I received a Purple Heart and then was discharged.

Interviewer: So you were given the Purple Heart?

Carl: Yes. I'm proud of my service, but I was so glad to get out of there alive. Many in my unit didn't.

Carl's story of life in the service is dominated by the horrors of Vietnam. Like other black veterans of this era, he describes being forced into compromising experiences that he attributes to race. For one, Carl describes both the most degrading and dangerous jobs being routinely assigned to soldiers of color. Although race may not speak to the broader alienation of the combat veteran, many black veterans I interviewed describe being frequently degraded by white superiors. This deep mistrust between black soldiers and white officers is especially pervasive in the experience of Vietnam era veterans' documented not only here but in prior research.[1] As we will see, AVF soldiers also describe being racially stereotyped by their white superiors as disproportionately aggressive, insubordinate, and even dangerous.

"WE WERE IN COMBAT AND WE DIDN'T HAVE TIME FOR THAT KIND OF BS"

When Mel arrived in the staging area in Da Nang in the middle of monsoon season, it was raining harder than anything he had ever seen. Before he knew it, he was on a chopper with four others and knew he was about to begin his tour as a combat Marine. After training, Mel was shipped directly to Vietnam.

Interviewer: What was it like when you first got there?

Mel: When we landed, I knew I was in Vietnam. Shit, as soon as the chopper hit the ground it was on its way up. It ain't waiting for nobody! So you jump out of this thing fast. And the mud was up to my knees. And that's when I said, "Oh shit, I'm in for it now!"

Interviewer: What were the daily conditions like?

Mel: We were located in a place we called "the fishbowl." We were dug in between a razorback and a rock pile. [Base Camp] is about ten miles from us. The DMZ [Demilitarized Zone] was less than a mile from us. That's where I was the entire time I was over there.

Mel described serving with a racially diverse squad. I asked if this posed any challenges. In describing the group, Mel talks about a serious conflict he had with one of two white soldiers from West Virginia.

Interviewer: So you guys were pretty diverse. Did this pose any challenges?

Mel: My squad had eight guys. We had two blacks, one Mexican, one Samoan, one Native American, and two whites. And we got along except for me and this white guy from West Virginia. He didn't like me and I didn't like him. It was absolutely a racial thing. It was my first experience in my life with racism. This guy took a shot at me on search and destroy mission. But me and the dude behind him kicked his ass. And after that I had no problem with him. He stayed in my squad until the end.

Interestingly, despite growing up in a racially segregated urban neighborhood, Mel describes his first real encounter with racism as occurring in Vietnam. As Mel's tour progressed, he describes other racial tensions he experienced with whites.

Interviewer: So it was only with this one white soldier from West Virginia? Were there other racial conflicts between white and black soldiers that you remember?

Mel: Yes. Here's one story that's as clear as day to me. So, we were on top of this rock pile. There were three squads positioned up there. And it was tough because we were climbing straight up it seemed like. And there was a white guy who gave me a hard time, and we got in a bare knuckle brawl right there.

Interviewer: What happened?

Mel: Well, after the fight we got called down into the lieutenant's tent. And the white guy went in first and was in there for about a minute. Then I got in there and he looks at me and says, "Let me tell you what, I don't like no niggers in my Marine Corps." And I said, "Okay then, I guarantee that you will be dead tomorrow," and I walked right out. And I went down and told the guys in my squad, and they were like let's get him now. And I was like, "No, no let's wait." We'll give him a chance to get off of this mountain. And he was gone. He wasn't on there the next day. . . . I mean, we were in combat and we didn't have time for that kind of BS.

In addition to a conflict with a racist white officer, Mel also described black soldiers being disproportionately assigned the worst jobs. Here, Mel describes a situation after he was sent to the rear area after many months on the front lines.

Interviewer: What did they have you doing back there?

Mel: You know, when I got injured and came back to the rear area, we were just resting and then sitting around waiting. But then I started to notice the way things went down back

> there and it wasn't pretty. Once we were able to recover and able to move around, all the black troops were stuck cleaning shitters. And I did that a lot, too much [laughs]. But we had to empty them and put all of it in a pit, stir in the kerosene, and burn it up. I couldn't be back there with that kind of treatment. I actually begged to go back into the field, and fortunately they put me back out there pretty quickly.

Mel's remaining time in Vietnam would, however, be over soon. Approximately ten months after he arrived in country he got infected with malaria. Mel was very hazy with the details. Indeed, he remembers only that he was given leave shortly after his diagnosis.

Interviewer: So you got malaria and then you were given a leave. Tell me what happened?

Mel: All I know is that it happened just as we was going out on a company-size search and destroy mission. We probably got maybe about two hundred yards from our compound, and I went out like a light. . . . Boom! Just went out, Jack. Next thing I know is I'm waking up, and I got this big hand in my face. . . . So, I'm trying to move to get away from it and somebody's holding me back. And they were telling me I was in a helicopter, and I guess I lost it. I'm thinking I'm still on the ground and the enemy is on top of me. But they finally calmed me down, got somebody to give me a shot. And I felt better.

After this incident, Mel's time in Vietnam would come to an end. However, he would continue to suffer terribly from malaria. Indeed, Mel's illness pushed him perilously close to death.

Interviewer: So were you eventually sent back to your unit?

Mel: No. They needed somebody to go on R&R, but were concerned about my health. But I wanted to go to Japan. And sure as shit, I got sick over there. The only thing I remember is waking up in the hospital, say probably about two months later. I mean I was very, very sick and almost died.

Interviewer: But you recovered and then what?

Mel: They sent me home. It was December 24, 1967. Christmas Eve of 1967.

Interviewer: Wow, a Christmas you'll never forget.

Mel: Yeah, it was a crazy time over there, but I was happy to be home with my family.

"BLACK SOLDIERS WERE CALLED TO DO THE MOST DANGEROUS ASSIGNMENTS"

Another Vietnam veteran, Bobby—who was not forthcoming about his childhood and excluded from the previous chapter—welcomed the opportunity to speak about his time in the service. Bobby was also one of the few Vietnam era veterans who served in an elite combat unit. Therefore, his experience as a black soldier in a leadership role provides an important contrast with other Vietnam era respondents. Did being a black soldier in an elite unit make race irrelevant?

Bobby met me at one of IH's outdoor picnic tables. He arrived with a duffle bag full of service-related mementos that he had saved. He proudly showed me his picture in a dress uniform. Bobby's picture was of a proud soldier in a beret, whose lapel was stacked with service medals. As we began to talk about his experience in the military, Bobby first informed me that, "I couldn't divulge everything, because it still hasn't been debriefed." After I informed Bobby that I wasn't necessarily interested in the very particulars of his combat service, he appeared at ease and our interview began.

Interviewer: So tell me about your experience in Vietnam.

Bobby: It was intense. I mean, here I am in my twenties, and given the responsibility of an entire squad. You learn quick, especially when you're responsible for ten or fifteen lives.

After he explained to me some of the more technical aspects of his service in Vietnam, I asked him if race ever played a role in his combat experience.

Bobby: I think it was pretty clear that black soldiers in my unit were the ones who were called to do the most dangerous assignments. I didn't think anything of it, because I was up for the job. But it was pretty damn obvious. We were always having to prove ourselves one way or another.

Interviewer: Was it only in the assignments you were given, or were there other ways you felt like race was part of your experience?

Bobby: Ha! When isn't race a part of your experience? I mean look at IH, you see any white faces here besides your own?

Interviewer. Good point.

Bobby: I'm just messing with you. . . . I think the military really brings it out. It's just presumed a black soldier doesn't have the intelligence to lead. So you gotta let your actions do the talking. But one thing I do remember, especially later on into my tour, was some anti-war stuff happening. We'd be walking down the trail and find these leaflets that said something like, "My black brother, why are you fighting your brother. It's not your war; come to our side."

Interviewer: What kind of impact did those make on you?

Bobby: None whatsoever. I was too busy doing my job to think much about it. . . . I really didn't think about that stuff. You know, the mistreatment of Vietnam vets, until after I got back home from Vietnam.

Interviewers: What about with your superiors? Was there anything blatantly racist that went on?

Bobby: Not anything too blatant or racist. . . . But I mean there were times when a group of black soldiers were on an ambush and we come back the next day. And I'd be debriefed and asked to share in detail with my superiors everything that we had been through—lost a lot of good men over there—and you'd think, "We're going to get a day off." But I don't remember ever getting one. White soldiers definitely got time off, no question about it. We'd come back shot up or whatever and they'd be lying around waiting for us. So, we knew it was racial—it was unspoken—but it was obvious what was going on. . . . Like I said, we just had to keep driving on, it was kill or be killed over there. Thankfully, all my training paid off, and I was one of the lucky ones to come home.

The differential treatment toward black soldiers that Bobby describes is echoed by many of the black Vietnam era veterans I interviewed. What is interesting in Bobby's account is his articulation of institutional racism in practice. The "unspoken" but clear message was that black soldiers were not worthy of downtime, even those who served in an elite combat unit. At the same time, throughout his interview, Bobby was careful not to complain. His phrase, "Keep driving on," is a code common to all those in the military, but for Bobby this meant more than being resilient to the horrors of war. It also was a means for dealing with the differential treatment he experienced within the ranks of his own unit. Bobby next shared a horrific story about his last mission in Vietnam:

> Before we went out to the field on patrol or a mission I always prayed. My prayers were directed toward not losing anybody. On this particular day that I got injured, and the point man was killed by what you call a "Bouncing Betty" [a small mine set off by trip wires], I was just behind him. And when I heard the popping sound I knew immediately what it was, so I turned to run and got everybody back and down. What I didn't realize until we got back was that it tore half of my foot off.

Bobby stayed in a military hospital for about four months before he returned stateside. When I asked him to offer any last reflections on his combat experience, his voice turned very somber:

> I've done things that I regret—shoot first, ask questions later— that kind of thing. But sometimes you know when you're in the field you can't wait for backup, you gotta act. I mean we got to keep moving. Even if that means shooting our way through, because sometimes it seemed we were waiting for airpower forever. We were left with no choice.

"I LOST EVERYTHING"

Upon being drafted into the Vietnam War, Lionel went straight from the projects of Baltimore to boot camp. He describes himself as "lucky" as he was deployed to Germany to provide supportive services and was never deployed to Vietnam. However, Lionel's description as "lucky" was not as accurate as being "unlucky" at getting sent to Vietnam, as the majority of drafted civilians were sent to support locations in other countries, and only a small percentage in Vietnam actually saw combat.[2] In contrast to other black Vietnam era veterans I interviewed, Lionel described his experience in the service during this period as far more racially inclusive:

> You see, my experience was that racist attitudes were squashed by the mission. The mission is one for a unit. If we are ordered to take a hill, you can't be racist about taking the hill, because you need that black guy or that southern white guy to assist you in taking that hill. So a lot of things were just put to the side when it came to the mission.

On the other hand, Lionel described his unit as essentially relegated to menial tasks such as KP (kitchen duty) and tedious garbage removal details. Interestingly, however, as his time in Germany went on, his unit, excluding officers, became almost entirely black. Lionel described this demographic change as resulting in fewer promotions. Overall, however, he believed it made his experience in the service much more positive:

> The more black we became, the more control we had. A negative situation became a positive. We were running the show! And as men with a strong bond to soul music, for example, we created little outlets for ourselves. For me, I could sing. So we formed our own little group. We did shows on base and stuff like that. So we adapted and made the best of the situation.

The above account is interesting as it reveals how black culture, or "home-frames" or "counter-frames,"[3] became an important way for Lionel's predominantly African-American unit to cope with being in the service. While Lionel described promotions as coming slow, under the circumstances, he didn't believe this was necessarily a bad thing. As he describes, promotions became far less attractive if it meant being transferred to Vietnam:

> We had our eyes on promotions, because we did want them. I mean they had new two young white guys come over who were instantly promoted from sergeant to buck sergeant over all of us who had been in rank a lot longer than they had. Well, I came to learn that they were reassigned and shipped to Vietnam! So, you know, in retrospect I feel that shit, I was mad that I didn't get the promotion. But you know after they got it, it was like, "Whoa, I'm so glad I didn't get it! Because there was no way that I wanted to go to Vietnam. I was perfectly content in Germany, thank you very much [laughs].

After returning from Germany to Baltimore, Lionel continued for three more years on the Inactive Ready Reserves (IRR) and then eventually reenlisted in the Army National Guard. Of all the African-American veterans that I interviewed, Lionel's experience with the GI Bill was by far the most positive. After returning to Baltimore, he was soon accepted into college and went on to receive both a bachelor's and a master's degree. During this time, Lionel also worked in a Baltimore alderman's office. It was there that the next phase of his military service would begin:

> Every summer my Army National Guard unit was doing summer camps in the woods up in Maryland. And then I met this guy who worked in an office on the floor below me who in the Air Force National Guard and he would tell me about his summers in Greece, Germany, Russia, Hawaii, Panama; I mean he was going all over the world. And here I am in the Army National Guard always going to the woods. So I said to myself, "Wait a minute, this guy's not that much smarter than me. Why is he going to all these amazing places and I'm not [laughs]?"

Lionel learned that a switch to the Air Guard would result in a loss of rank, so he decided to take nearly a year to weigh his options. However, he decided that "the army was the same old go to the woods and train stuff. So, I said okay, I'll take a reduction in rank. Fortunately, I found out that the reduction in rank would only last for about a year. . . . So I gave it a shot, I transferred over and the rest was history. I got to go around the world a couple of times."

At this time, Lionel was married with children. As a veteran, he took full advantage of both the VA's loan program to purchase a home and a low-interest loan to start his "dream" business by opening a music club. Lionel's military service put him on a remarkable trajectory, which he attributes to a passion for learning and also his love for music. By the luck of the draw, Lionel was able to hone his craft during his time in Germany during the Vietnam era. And in subsequent years, his ultimate dream of opening a music club finally came true. I was therefore shocked by what he told me next:

Interviewer: So after you opened the music club did you get out of the service?

Lionel: No, I stayed in the Air Guard until last year.

Interviewer: Was that ever challenging trying to balance your obligations as a club owner?

Lionel: Um. . . . Yeah. . . . Because of my military commitments in the 1990s—I served in Operation Desert Storm—I had to leave and as a result of me leaving, I lost my business and my collateral was my home, so I lost my home as well. I mean, I lost everything.

Interviewer: Oh gosh . . . .

Lionel: Yeah. . . . I'm over in the desert and obviously not able to manage the business—you go to war—so I had some people I thought I could trust to manage it, but it didn't work out that way. So, I tried to pour some money into it to try to resurrect it, but it was too little too late. . . . I was smart enough to get an attorney to advise me on what I needed to do. . . . I was smart about it.

Interviewer: So you were able to rebound once you got an attorney?

Lionel: Yeah, but it took some time. I was broke and so I went to Small Business Administration and asked them for advice and they blew me off. So, it was very hard . . . . I think that was my lowest point, trying to deal with that, so I was like Kenny Rogers, I knew when to hold 'em and when to fold 'em.

Interviewer: So you filed for bankruptcy?

Lionel Yup, but I was able to stay above water with help from loved ones and I stayed in the Air Guard, so I had some pay coming in.

Still trying to manage his extremely difficult financial situation with loans from family and pay from the military, Lionel's troubles at home would soon be put on hold. His luck would change dramatically after September 11, 2001. Like other black veterans of Operation Iraqi Freedom such as Andre, this unprecedented historical moment energized Lionel to serve: "I was ready to go over there and do my job for a cause that I, like most Americans at the time, believed in." While Lionel had some experience in Operation Desert Storm with the challenges of wartime duties, it was not nearly as viscerally traumatic as the far costlier war in Iraq. Lionel's unit was assigned the awful job of loading corpses onto planes heading back to the United States, something he experienced previously in Operation Desert Storm. However, the death toll in Iraq was far greater and took a major toll on Lionel.

Interviewer: Tell me about your experience in Iraq.

Lionel: It was crazy. There was so much death. The casualty counts kept us at it all hours of the day. The hours were incredibly long. And you gotta understand, I'm almost sixty at the time, so it was physically grueling too. I mean, loading body after body. And it was chaos over there in Iraq. I mean during Desert Storm, we had many officers and it was well organized. Iraq was a beast. It was fewer people, harder work, and total confusion about our hours. The truth is, we pretty much didn't stop working, and there was no one we could call on for relief. But we got it done, and I'm back and now retired.

Lionel's career in the military spanned nearly four decades. While he was comparatively lucky in that he avoided combat duty in Vietnam, an unexpected turn of events would lead him into an unforgiving environment in Iraq. Having lost his business and home, Lionel stayed in the military to survive. Sadly, the experience in Iraq has resulted in PTSD, and even though he is now retired from the military, he describes his current economic situation as "very difficult. I'm still broke, but somehow able to hold on." On top of it all, Lionel described being plagued by nightmares of "endless piles of corpses, death everywhere." But he also takes solace when he visits the VA: "You wouldn't believe all the young people with missing limbs and maimed; it's Vietnam all over again . . . . So I got out of the service pretty lucky, when I think about it."

"MY CAPTAIN WAS THIS REDNECK RACIST FROM GEORGIA"

Earl also had the luck of the draw and was sent to Germany. In contrast to Lionel, however, he described his experience in the infantry as much more racially divisive.

Interviewer: Tell me about Germany, were there any racial tensions in your unit?

Earl: My captain was this redneck racist from Georgia. And in not so many words, he told us that he did not like blacks. I mean they put us on latrine duty all the time. I felt like all the blacks lived in the shitters [laughter].

In addition to this racially degrading experience, Earl's situation as compared to other respondents was particularly hostile. Here, he describes an experience in which black soldiers were arbitrarily held responsible for the beating of a white sergeant:

> There was a white sergeant who got beaten up and they tried to pin it on me and three other black soldiers. We got court-martialed and faced twenty years in the brig, but we were acquitted. And then just after that, this the captain called us into his quarters. And I'll never forget Top [first sergeant] said, "Go back out there and salute the captain the right way, boy!" And the Captain told me, "You may have gotten away with this, but I ain't done with you yet. I'm gonna get your ass." So he would send guys to fuck with us. I mean, he wanted me to take a swing at one of them, so I would be put in the brig. But I sucked it up and made it home.

Earl also provided important insight into the challenges he experienced as a black soldier "coming out of the projects." Specifically, he found strength in the bond he was able to maintain.

Interviewer: How did the other soldiers react to black soldiers from the north?

Earl: There were southern white dudes. They weren't all racists, but they saw us as gangsters.

Interviewer: How did you deal with them?

Earl: I mean all black soldiers identified with each other. We stuck together and supported one another, although, we drank a lot and later on, for me, that wasn't a good thing . . . to say the least. But thank the lord for my brothers. I wouldn't have made without the support.

Despite the challenges he experienced as a black solider, however, Earl described his overall experience in the military very positively:

> Well, you know, I actually think I learned more about being a man in the military than anywhere else. I learned that you have to persevere no matter what the situation. There was a lot of BS they put black soldiers through, but it thickened your skin. I still today believe that whatever doesn't kill me, makes me stronger.

Earl's experience in the military was marked by a visceral climate of white racial hostility. After escaping court-martial, a racist white superior officer continued to try and torment Earl and other black soldiers. Earl believed that the white officer's strategy was to have antagonized him into a likely court-martial and negative discharge. Yet he was able to avoid such confrontations by adopting a survivalist orthodoxy. Indeed, such a discipline would be an ever increasing part of Earl's post-military life. Yet survival for Earl as a veteran would not result in the kind of positive outcome he describes when he was discharged from the military. Earl's words, "Whatever doesn't kill me, makes me stronger," is perhaps his way of sharing a view that is especially relevant to his post-military experiences (see chapter 5).

"THE FACT THAT I WAS BLACK MIGHT HAVE BEEN A COINCIDENCE, BUT I DOUBT IT"

After he enlisted to avoid the draft, Vietnam era veteran Otis became a data processing specialist and was sent to training for a year and a half before being shipped out to Vietnam. Why he remained stateside for as long as he did remained a mystery to Otis. For one, he was the only member of his unit not to be assigned to a data processing unit.

Interviewer: So what would they have you do?

Otis: I played limo driver for these officers. . . . There were like three of us black drivers. None of them were data processors, but we were put together doing this shit. If it wasn't racial, it sure as hell felt like it. Especially considering that the rest of my unit were doing what they had been trained to do as data processors. Now the fact that I was black might have been a coincidence, but I doubt it. I would have thought that even if I wasn't going to go to Vietnam, I would be doing data processing. That's what I was trained to do. But I was stuck there for a year and half as a chump driver.

Interviewer: How did that make you feel?

Otis: I was pissed. I mean I should be with my data processing unit. It was a waste of my time and energy. And then I kept complaining to senior level officers, "You need to get me the hell out of here, I'm trained to do data processing." And then I was eventually sent to a data processing unit in Vietnam—Long Bien right outside of Saigon—I was finally running programs.

Once in country, Otis had limited exposure to combat. However, he recalled one experience on night patrol:

> I mean, we heard a lot of explosions. And the VC got close to the line, so we were sent out on all night patrol. It was scary. I mean any time your daily routine is thrown off like that, you know this is serious business.

Otis explains that his religious faith was key for coping in such times.

Otis: I always had the feeling that no matter what, I'm going get through this. This too shall pass. This is God sending you a message. . . . I truly believe that I'm blessed. I mean look, I made it home from Vietnam without a scratch.

Interviewer: Where did that faith come from?

Otis: Oh definitely, my upbringing. My faith was always strong but never stronger than in Vietnam.

Perhaps similar to Earl, Otis recounting his war experience is as much or more a reflection of his incredibly challenging post-war experiences. Indeed, it is likely that Otis's description of faith as providing him strength in Vietnam is tied to the role of religion in his life today. In the next chapter, it becomes clear how survival through faith has played a tremendously important role in Otis's prolonged struggles with addiction.

"NO MATTER WHAT, BLACKS NEEDED TO SHUT THE HELL UP AND DO WHAT WE'RE TOLD"

Charles's experience leaving Wilmington for the service was at a time of sudden and often explosive racial upheaval in the United States. It was the summer of 1968, just after Dr. Martin Luther King Jr.'s assassination. After basic training, Charles took a final leave to say good-bye to his family before being shipped off to Vietnam. Returning to a city utterly transformed by explosive race riots and martial law was an absolute shock to Charles. Interestingly, he was utterly oblivious to the circumstances until *after* he returned to Wilmington.

Interviewer: So you were able return one last time to Wilmington before shipping out?

Charles: Yeah, I came back to Wilmington on the bus, and the place was a ghost town. I didn't know where everybody went. But I had my duffel bag and I'm walking down the street and this jeep pulls up—National Guard jeep—and the dude says, "Where are you going?" And then he asks me, "You're in the military?" And I said, "Yeah." And he says, "What you doing walking around this time of night? Don't you know that this whole city is under martial law?" And, I said, "Nope, don't know anything about it."

Based on his own experience at the time, Charles believed race riots were only occurring in the south, including on the military base where he completed his basic training.

Interviewer: Were you at all aware of the racial unrest after Dr. King's murder while you were in training?

Charles: Oh yeah, there were these race riots after Dr. King's assassination on base and in the city, but I didn't know they were going on up here in Wilmington. Everyone knew about it down south. I was in training when a riot on base actually started. There were microphones all over the post and the announcement comes on, "Attention! Attention! The honorable Martin Luther King has just been assassinated." And then all the brothers came out in the open and were like, "Did you hear that? They killed King! They killed King!" Then the white guys were saying "Good enough for the nigger." And the brothers went off. We had our entrenchment tools out [small metal shovel] and every one of us were banging them together "Clang! Clang! Clang!" And then they called in the MPs [military police].

Interviewer: Wow, so how did they maintain order?

Charles: I mean there were no fires set like up in Wilmington, but there was a whole lot of brawling between blacks and whites all over the post. It was crazy. And I was scared. I mean I'm only eighteen and just trying to stay out of

> trouble. But I just stayed in the back, and we were ordered back in the barracks. A lot of people were going to the hospital; beat up really bad.

Once back in Wilmington, Charles arrived home to an empty house. His foster parents had gone on vacation to Niagara Falls, so he invited all of his friends from the neighborhood over for one last going away party. Charles describes how his return to base unfolded into a harrowing night of white racist turmoil that he described as "unforgettable":

Interviewer: So I bet you struggled to get back to the bus?

Charles: Oh yeah, the next day I had to be up early. So when I got on the bus, I'm still drunk [laughs]. And then I just passed out on the bus.

Interviewer: When did you wake up?

Charles: Somewhere in Raleigh, North Carolina. . . . I mean it must have be like three or four o'clock in the morning. And I get off the bus and cleared my throat and spit on the ground. And this white guy at the bus terminal says "Hey nigger! What you doing nigger?" And I'm in my uniform and I say, "Who the fuck do you think you're talking to? You better get back in that terminal motherfucker, or I'm going to bust you upside the head!" I mean that's the attitude I had back then, you know? But any way I'm looking around up at the bus terminal and there were maybe three black guys sweeping up, who worked there, and they all looked at me and then cowered in the corner. They were probably thinking, "This guy is crazy, he don't know what he's doing." And they were right, because the next thing I know this pick-up truck pulls up with like three or four big white boys. And the old man comes out and tells them about "this nigger spitting on the ground." You know, "Niggers don't do that stuff around here." And then one of the guys in the truck pulls out a baseball bat and says, "Where are you from nigger?" And I say, "I'm from Delaware." He says, "I don't care which bus comes next, but you better get your black ass on it or you're a dead motherfucker." And then they came up over the top of me yelling, "Get that spit up, nigger!" So I start cleaning it up with my hands in the dirt. And I'm crying. I am totally humiliated. And then a bus pulls up and I ask, "Shit, how much is it?" and he says, "Four dollars and seventy-five cents," and thank god I had

> a five dollar bill in my pocket or I would've been dead. Fortunately, the bus's next stop was the base. But I remember looking out the window at those guys and they're laughing and shouting "nigger!" I remember that now like it was yesterday. I'll never forget that. It's not something you forget.

When Charles returned to Ft. Bragg, South Carolina he described a distinct change in the racial consciousness of other black soldiers. Many had decided that they were not going to serve. They stood in solidarity against the callous treatment they had received in the wake of Dr. King's assassination. In fact, many black recruits at this time went AWOL. Charles describes this distinct change in attitude:

Interviewer: So things had really changed among the black recruits?

Charles: Yeah, we were betrayed. They kill this great American and use it as a way to treat us as scum of the earth. They don't even have the decency to acknowledge this tragedy. But that's how it was back then: No matter what, blacks needed to shut the hell up and do what we're told.

Interviewer: How were you able to cope?

Charles: I hung in there for a few more weeks and then a bunch of us went AWOL. I mean, I just had enough of all this. And you got to understand there were a lot of blacks—I remember actually it being nearly all blacks I trained with. We all deserted. But I didn't get any brig time, just a lot of KP—for like two weeks—and an official reprimand for desertion. They took my rank away, but I had so little that it didn't much matter. In terms of pay, they could bust me down any lower [laughs]!

Like several of the veterans I interviewed, Charles went into the service with a group of friends he grew up with from his neighborhood with the deep desire to serve together. But after deployment, in no instance were hometown friendship networks kept intact. Once in country, Charles's job involved extremely dangerous inventorying of ammunition. While he had heard of other ammo dumps being hit that resulted in many casualties, fortunately his unit never took any direct fire. I asked Charles about race relations in Vietnam.

Interviewer: Was there racial division among the troops you served with?

Charles:	Just like in training, black troops stayed together. We looking out for ourselves. We had a black first sergeant who really looked out for us. He let it be known to other troops not to mess with us. But that didn't last because he got transferred and our next first sergeant was white. He looked at us like we were shit and treated us like shit.
Interviewer:	How so?
Charles:	If you were a minute late you'd get written up or get stuck cleaning latrines.
Interviewer:	I've heard that before. Did you have any other experiences with racism or racial tensions in Vietnam?
Charles:	Oh yeah, there was this big white dude from the Ozarks. He hated niggers with a passion, and he was also definitely suffering from shell shock. . . . He wasn't stable and would confront you in your face, "Nigger, you got a problem? What are you looking at nigger?" I remember one day someone told us just stay away from him. But one brother didn't get the word and just said to him, "Hey, how you doing?" And he said "What did you say nigger?" And he went off and just started beating the guy. And it took about six or seven brothers to pull him off of him.

Like life on the base in the wake of Dr. King's assassination, Charles describes unity between black soldiers as an important part of his ability to persevere in such hostile conditions. He describes even very subtle interactions between black soldiers involving facial and hand gestures that symbolized racial solidarity as very comforting.

Interviewer:	Was that just waving to one another?
Charles:	Yeah, but also the "double V" sign [showing me]. Back then you put two Vs in the air: One for victory over here, and one for justice at home.
Interviewer:	That must have been supportive.
Charles:	It felt good to have that kind of pride in our struggle both here and at home. It kept us going, but I also know the whites didn't like it. But it felt good to know we had each other's backs.

After Vietnam, Charles was stationed in Okinawa where he would eventually be promoted to the rank of sergeant. This was no small achievement for Charles, indeed, as he describes in his overall impressions of serving in the military:

> I mean, I went a long way. None of it was easy. But I take great pride in my achievements and my time in the service. Overall, I had a hell of time. Man, I wish I would have stayed in. I mean by the time I made sergeant, I had it all going for me. But I didn't see it that way then—I was still young and stupid—so I only did one reenlistment, and then got out.

Charles's story of military service provides a window into how the war at home spilled over into the war abroad. Consider his first visit home to Wilmington. After conscription Charles witnessed intense race riots at Ft. Bragg but was utterly oblivious to the fact that his home city was under prolonged National Guard occupation. Moreover, Charles's story of his bus ride back to Ft. Bragg is more than a story of an individual's experience with southern white racism. It is a collective memory of a time when all aspects of civilian life were fraught with the possibility of lethal racial violence. It is thus not surprising that in the wake of Dr. King's murder, black soldiers all across the country banned together in acts of official resistance. While most engaged only in temporary desertion, the act itself reinforced a powerful sense of racial pride. Indeed, the fires of racial solidarity ignited on the home front by acts of white racism provided crucial symbolic capital that black Vietnam era veterans such as Charles could employ once they entered the war zone.

MILITARY SERVICE IN THE LIVES OF AVF ERA VETERANS: "THEY HAD COME TO SEE ME AS A THUG"

The intense climate of white racism and violence during the busing protests of the late 1970s led to Gerald's expulsion and subsequent enlistment in the air force. While Gerald's mother was a black nationalist and a strong critic of the American military, she accepted Gerald's decision as "not the navy, which I first considered. She was not happy about that, so when I came home and told my mom I'm going in the air force, she was okay with that." Gerald explains that he believed, especially given the numerous fights he got into in his last year of high school, that his family did not have high expectations that he'd have a successful career in the military.

Interviewer: What was that like going from such a chaotic several months of violence and upheaval in your life almost directly into the military?

Gerald:	Well, let's just say that my family was pretty sure that I wasn't going to make it through boot camp [laughs].
Interviewer:	So, how did that go?
Gerald:	You know but boot camp was not that bad for me. Air force boot camp was different than the army and the navy. There was no, "Down and give me twenty" kind of harsh discipline. You don't get that in the air force.

Gerald excelled in his training and became a radio operator. He graduated near the top of his class and was given one of the better duty assignments.

Interviewer:	Where were you stationed after training?
Gerald:	San Diego. I mean, you always hear about California as the place to be when you're coming up through training, and so that's where I wanted to be. So, I felt like things were working out well for me.

Gerald excelled in his job, was promoted quickly, and became a designated radio operations trainer very quickly. However, the fast track he was on generated a backlash among his supervisors in general and racial animosity by a white supervisor:

> I can remember learning that the shift supervisors and assistant supervisors got together and wrote a letter to our flight commander about their so called "problem" with me becoming a designated trainer so quickly. It was obvious there were racial tensions involved in that meeting. One supervisor in particular was a real racist cat. He tried everything he could to really get me busted.. . . For instance, when someone came in for the next shift and could take over one of the stations, all the operators, who happened to be white, could go. Well, without fail he had me wait until the whole shift had ended. And once he gave me a letter of counseling and told me to sign it! What did you think I was born last night!? I refused to sign it. You know, he just did all kind of things to mess with me. . . , He was crazy. So, I finally went and complained to this master sergeant who was actually my mentor, and he's a white guy. He told me to document everything this guy does to me, and when this escalates he'll be the one to bite the dust. And it happened, sure enough, he pulled my chair out from under me, so I jumped up—I wanted to beat the hell out of him—but went straight down to the front desk to the security booth and I told them, "My supervisor just assaulted me." Next thing I hear are sirens and they locked him up! It was beautiful. They came in our secure location cuffed him up and took him away. And he got charged with abuse of power, dereliction of duty and the big one, one that really tripped me out, he got charged with being AWOL because when they arrested him he was not on shift where he was supposed to be, they really socked it to him [laughs]. They busted him down and they gave him a real crap job like packing classified records.

At the same time, the situation wasn't a positive one for Gerald. I asked him if his previous experiences with white racist violence had impacted him.

Interviewer: That must have been really hard for you to have been treated that way, especially given all you had previously been through.

Gerald: Yeah, it was hard. But I paid the consequences in high school. So I gritted my teeth and, like I said, made sure he was held accountable. But after that I was on edge around white officers. That's definitely true.

Despite these challenges, Gerald continued to excel and became a workaholic. Indeed, he didn't take his first leave until almost two years into his first duty assignment. Returning to his old neighborhood was an eye opening experience for Gerald.

Interviewer: What was it like being away so long?

Gerald: It was strange. Things were beginning to take a change for the worse. I mean it was early into the 80s so crack hadn't hit hard yet. Actually, it didn't blow up until after I got out of the air force a few years later. But some of the guys I grew up with were getting involved in a little street life, you could see the neighborhood and the housing starting to deteriorate. . . . Unemployment was real high and so the quality of life in the neighborhood was on the decline. . . . Section 8 housing was starting to spread. We were people that were on welfare and what have you, and you could see the change.

When I asked Gerald whether there was anything about his return home that really stuck with him, he paused and then stated:

> Well, I really remember what my mom said to me. She had her ear to the ground and knew that what I was witnessing was a major collapse going on in our city. Basically she knew that the black community had been screwed and it was only going to get worse. And she told me that if I had not gone in the air force, I probably would be in jail like some of my buddies who already were having more serious run-ins with the police and what have you. I mean living in Wilmington as a young black man, especially after Reagan took over, you really had a target on your back.

After a year of training in Turkey, Gerald's next duty assignment could not have been more different than San Diego. Rather than organizing training and office work, he was assigned to a mobile communications team that provided radio support for other government agencies. His transfer caused Gerald to genuinely consider a long-term career in the military.

Interviewer: Tell me about the new assignment.

Gerald: It was amazing, and that's when I planned that the air force was going to be my permanent career. First of all, I was no longer a radio operator but an armed courier. And I was able to travel all over the world. . . .I mean I always loved being a free spirit and this seemed like the ultimate gig for me.

Unbeknownst to Gerald at the time, however, a courier trip to Honduras would involve his participation in activities he was completely unprepared for:

> I can remember I was in the communications trailer—and I was due to ship out that afternoon; it was in the morning—and I hear from a major that they needed snipers, and I found out he was talking directly to me. He explained that troops were gonna fire bomb the front of this camp, and we'll be up on the hill and were ordered to pop anyone who runs out the back. I shot many of them. And it was all in the name of the so-called war on drugs. . . . it was bullshit. . . . I mean, I was twenty-one years old and it was traumatizing, to say the least. It changed me forever.

The roller-coaster ride that characterized a relatively short period of time in Gerald's career is important to summarize. After returning home to a neighborhood that he began to no longer recognize—a time characterized by skyrocketing black unemployment and an ever more aggressive law enforcement presence in urban communities of color—Gerald found himself in a position defending from abroad the very drug war he witnessed tearing away at the fabric of his community. Next, I asked Gerald about his own personal reflections on Honduras:

Interviewer: Why would they send you there as a sniper?

Gerald: I honestly believe it was my background. I was smart, a good shot, but they had come to see me as a thug. Someone who could kill without conscience. It was absolutely fucked up. They had no business doing this to me, but it's exactly what they did. In their eyes, I was just another nigger.

Interviewer: What happened over the next period of your career?

Gerald:	Honduras came to define me. I was this courier thug now. They had me essentially going back and forth to Honduras and other places killing people. And as a courier there was never any warning. I was disposable, wherever they needed me to take someone out, they sent me.
Interviewer:	So what happened in the end of your career?
Gerald:	They sent me to Europe. But the damage was already done to me. Nightmares, sweats, the whole nine yards. So I eventually went AWOL.
Interviewer:	Were you court-martialed?
Gerald:	No, I mean, I think my officers knew how fucked up I was. I mean I was doing this solo and then I was put on a base somewhere. They knew what I was doing, but I was the only one in my unit ordered to do this stuff. So I had had enough of it, and got out.
Interviewer:	Were you debriefed?
Gerald:	Yeah, I was debriefed when it was finally decided that I was getting out. . . .The biggest shock was when I learned that none of the sniper-related stuff was ever gonna show up in my records. . . . Which has turned into a major problem for me, because the VA says there's nothing in my records that indicates that I should have PTSD, so to this day I still only receive very limited disability benefits.

"HE CALLED ME A NIGGER AND TOOK A SWING AT ME"

Gregory described his military training with enthusiasm. At the same time, returning home was a culture shock. Moreover, Gregory's relationship with his pregnant girlfriend dramatically changed. Now the father of a newborn son, he discovered that the situation had changed dramatically since he left for boot camp.

Interviewer:	So what were you like after you finished training?
Gregory:	Gung ho, man, I was in the best shape of my life. I was excited about active duty and ready to be career military.
Interviewer:	So what happened when you returned home to Wilmington?

Gregory: I was kind of surprised how strange the place was. I mean I was poor when I went—lived in the 'hood you know—but I really didn't like it there anymore. The hopelessness of the place really sunk in, you know? So I wanted back in the military. I mean, I don't know, there were possibilities there and ain't shit back here.

Interviewer: What happened with your girlfriend?

Gregory: When I got home she had already moved on. I think we both moved on, really. But she seemed tripped out by me, what I had become, real serious and intense. I was the father of my son, but I never knew my son, and I found out also that she was seeing someone else. I was pissed off, you know what I'm saying? But in my head, I had already moved on. Shit, as far I was concerned, I was military now and this was just a visit home.

But what about child support payments? I wondered how Gregory's return really meant that he could make the kind of clean break that he described. Apparently, "moving on" to Gregory also referred to his girlfriend's new partner as assuming the responsibilities as his newborn son's father.

Interviewer: How were you able to make child support arrangements with your impending career in the service and all?

Gregory: She had another guy looking after my son. So, at the time we ended things. I just made a clean break. But no problems with child support. Shit, I was twenty and broke. Child support was a big issue later on with another woman and child. But that didn't catch up with me until after I got out of the service.

Gregory's first duty station was in Panama soon after Operation Just Cause had begun. In contrast, to Vietnam era veterans, Gregory described his time in Panama as a whirlwind but, ultimately, a very positive experience.

Interviewer: What was Just Cause like?

Gregory: Very organized, we had steady patrols. . . . We knew our jobs. . . . It was a trip going straight to Panama out of training! I gotta tell you, I loved it.

Interviewer: Did you see any combat?

Gregory: No, we heard the blasts all over the place. But we were working the perimeter, so we never saw the enemy at all.

When I asked Gregory if he encountered any differential treatment because of his race, Gregory stated, "No, because my unit was mostly black. The officers were white and not out there with us and didn't sleep in tents with us, I'll tell you that much." It was not until several years later when Gregory got to his next duty station in Hawaii, that he recalls an overtly racist incident.

Interviewer: You mentioned problems with race in Hawaii; what happened?

Gregory: It was the beginning of the end for me. I was an E5 [sergeant] and left the military with no rank because another white NCO put his hands on me. I mean we kept to ourselves mostly—blacks over there, whites over here—that's the way it is everywhere, you know? But when this NCO crossed the line—we didn't like each other because of past disagreements—and he called me a nigger and took a swing at me, I swung back. And I got busted. That was it. I got tired of the bull, and I said you know what, I am getting out.

Gregory looks back with regret at how his situation turned out, as, like many other black vets I interviewed, he envisioned himself as having a lengthy career in the military. However, his new assignment after the altercation soured him to this idea.

Interviewer: Did you have regrets about getting out?

Gregory: I should have stayed, but I didn't. I would still be in there now if I had stayed. I thought the grass was greener out here. I said, "Oh man I'll go back to the world and make some money." But I didn't get how good it was for me in the military. I mean I was stationed in Hawaii! And had an easy job and it got easier after I got busted down to private. I beat up an NCO, and now I'm "Mr. Fix-It"—I was painting and replacing light bulbs and stuff. And I reported directly to the first sergeant—who had twenty-six years in and couldn't nobody say much to him. He would only call me if he needed me, so there was a lot of time off.

Gregory's decision to get out of the service was solidified after a car detailing business he started on the outside started to be profitable. After losing all his rank, it became clear that his new position as a handyman for a high ranking NCO lacked the challenge Gregory desired, although he started his own car detailing business on the side.

Interviewer: So you were on your own, but it sounds like you had found new interests?

Gregory: I was making more money detailing cars off base in Hawaii than I was getting from the army! So, I was like I can get out and do this! I said to first sergeant one day, "I can make more money at home than I can make here, so I'm not going to reenlist. And he said, "Well, you know the paper work better than I do." So I get everything signed and that was that. All the people did the little check off, finalized everything and got it done. And I gave it to Top [first sergeant] and he said, "Alright, are you sure this is what you wanna do this?" And I said, "I'm never here, I am always out there in paradise making money." I mean, why would I want to stay in the military at this point?

A racial altercation with a senior ranking white soldier led to a radical change in Gregory's military career. Like others, his time in the service seemed to be mostly positive. However, one fight meant a major demotion and loss in pay. Clearly, Gregory's primary concern was now a lack of financial capital. While he now regrets leaving the service, Gregory was able to start his own business. Although his post-military experience is fraught with challenges, it is interesting to note how his work ethic remained strong. Indeed, Gregory is one of the few homeless veterans I interviewed who had a concrete employment plan for the future (see chapter 4).

"I BECAME AWARE OF THE RACISM THING WHEN I STARTED GETTING REAL FRUSTRATED"

Recall from the previous chapter that Terrence was a veteran with a turbulent early childhood. After bouncing from one foster care home to another, he found himself destitute and in a special high school for troubled youth. He described his decision to join the military as quite frankly a way to avoid homelessness. Like Vietnam era veteran Lionel, Terrence had experiences in two different branches of the military. In contrast to Lionel's trajectory as draftee and then transfer to Air National Guard as means for seeing the world, Terrence's decision was driven by poverty, joblessness, and survival. He began his military career in the early 1980s in the army as part of a field artillery unit stationed in Korea.

Interview: Tell me about Korea.

Terrence: It was crazy. I loved it over there. But we went overboard with the drinking and brawling. I mean, I was fresh out of high school and had never experienced anything like it, so, let's just say I was in over my head [laughs].

Interviewer: How so?

Terrence: Well, I was used to always facing consequences for my actions—surviving in and out foster homes and what have you—but active duty there was no one that gave us younger ones any advice on life skills. So, being in the service was like the streets to me—it's all about respect. You know, putting up a big front. But I could hang with that. It was the alcohol and drugs that I couldn't handle and it became a big problem, plus at the time I didn't know it, but I was suffering from serious depression

Terrence's substance abuse problems and mental illness would plague his entire military career. When it came to race relations, Terrence described a mistrust of both white and black soldiers in his unit.

Interviewer: Were there racial tension you experienced?

Terrence: I mean there were factions across racial lines. We had to watch ourselves around white officers—I mean, we knew they were looking for any little thing to get us out. And also black soldiers that we called "lifers." They were loyal to whatever the army wanted and would rat your ass out in a second. And my group well, we just wanted to do our time, party, and move on. But it got ugly really fast. . . . It was crazy. . . . I mean we'd go into clubs off base and what not and someone in our group was always getting in trouble, but fortunately I was able to make it out in one piece.

Terrence actually considered getting out of the military at this point, but after a leave to Wilmington he discovered his employment options were very limited. Moreover, similar to other AVF era black veterans, he described his neighborhood as noticeably deteriorating. Increased police presence, substandard living conditions, and especially lack of employment opportunities made reenlisting in his words "a no brainer."

Interviewer: Tell me why you waited to reenlist after you got out of the service after Korea?

Terrence: I had nothing good waiting for me back in the 'hood. And when I say nothing, I mean it. Shit, people were hurting—I mean dying—when I got back. . . . And not much had

> changed with work. . . . I mean, there were no good jobs. Shit, even my brothers had left for the south because of how bad it was. But I wasn't too tight with them, so I thought I'd go back home to Wilmington. But it was ugly—a deadend—you know what I'm saying?

After reenlisting, Terrence was sent to his next duty station. Now stationed back in the United States on a base that he described as "pretty plain, but good enough," he tried to turn the military into a long-term career. However, his experiences would take a dramatic turn for the worse. Here, he explains the events precipitating this downward spiral.

Interviewer: You mentioned things "not lasting." What happened in the army?

Terrence: It started when we went into the wrong bar, it was this place with all white local yokels, but we were headstrong military and not going to leave. I'm not sure what words were exchanged, but one of my buddies was getting jumped by a bunch of these fools. . . . [Fortunately,] I was able to beat some of 'em off of him and got my buddy free—I grabbed him and we took off running—and made it to my car.

Terrence chalked this experience up "to being dumb and in over our heads; we shouldn't have even gone into that place." However, this situation had far more negative repercussions than he might have imagined. Upon return to the base, both Terrence and his friend were formally reprimanded. They lost rank, were assigned monotonous work details, and required to take a substance abuse prevention course. Fortunately, they escaped formal court-martial proceedings.

Interviewer: What happened as the result of the reprimand?

Terrence: We lost rank and that meant less pay. But I think after this I started to develop a bad reputation. No one trusted me. We had to take some alcohol and drug classes. But I was really battling anxiety and depression at that point. I was having panic attacks. . . . And I started drinking too much. It's like after that one night I went from being good 'ol Terry to someone people avoided like the plague.

I asked Terrence if the sanctions were similar for other soldiers in his situation. Here, it became clear that race was an issue that Terrence perceived as almost certainly resulting in a loss of rank. He described witnessing white soldiers getting away with far more serious violations and never once witnessing a loss of rank or being subjected to the kind of alienation he experienced. Terrence believed that his white superiors operated on a double standard when it came to how they treated black soldiers.

Interviewer: Tell me why you believed there was a double standard for black soldiers?

Terrence: I became aware of the racism thing when I started getting real frustrated. My temper was short to begin with, but anything I tried to say fell on deaf ears. And it's obvious that once you is marked like I was, that you got some of these racist white guys—guys with rank that have had enough of the loud black pissant—they want to burn you if you is black, because they intimidated and they don't want to listen to anything you gotta say.

Interviewer: So how would they try to burn you?

Terrence: For stupid reasons, they'd try to set us off, so we'd get kicked out, be barred from reenlisting. . . . I was totally aware of that, but I tried to ignore it and just do my job. But I also had a lot of pain inside, and no one wants to hear about that in the military. It's a weakness to show emotion.

Indeed, Terrence describes this climate of racial hostility as characterized by a violent masculinity similar to what Richard Majors and Janet Billson term the "cool pose."[4] Similar to black men in ghettoized communities, marginalized black male soldiers such as Terrence go to extreme lengths to conceal their emotions, because they are viewed as weakness. However, Terrence's own problems with untreated mental illness and substance abuse were making his experience in the military especially volatile. Apparently, as the next exchange reveals, Terrence began to feel even more depressed and alienated, which in turn resulted in a continued abuse of alcohol. Indeed, he became more withdrawn and the sanctions he received were severe.

Interviewer: It sounds like things were starting to really become difficult for you. How did things end?

Terrence: I got burned. A white sergeant who had his eye on me 24/7, caught me sleeping on duty. And I had like three weeks left in the military. They put me on extra duty, and they busted my rank down, and they tried to prevent me from reenlisting. They gave me a piece of paper. And on the back of the sheet of paper it said, "Why do you think that you should not be barred from reenlisting?" And I just wrote on there that I have not done anything to be barred from reenlisting. And that it didn't make any sense.

Interviewer: So they didn't throw you out?

Terrence: No, they didn't throw me out. But I was fed up so I got discharged and came home.

Interviewer: So did you enlist in the marines right away?

Terrence: No, I got my truck driver's license and tried to get work back in Wilmington.

Terrence soon realized that for a young man in his early twenties, especially in a tough Reagan-era economy that it was difficult to maintain steady work. Once again Terrence was faced with a choice: enlist in the military or become destitute. While his mother and stepfather were still in the city, he described having little to no contact with them.

Interviewer: Did you have any family who could help you out?

Terrence: No, I saw my mom. But I've been on my own for so long and still can't deal with my stepdad, so I stay away. I'm a loner.

Interviewer: Where did you stay?

Terrence: At the YMCA for a little while. And then my brother moved back, so I stayed on his couch until it was time to move on from that.

Interviewer: So once again you needed a change?

Terrence: Yup. And I always looked up to the Marine Corps, so I enlisted.

After finishing boot camp at Paris Island, Terrence's first duty station was stateside where he worked as a mechanic. However, only a few months into his enlistment, Terrence's untreated mental illness and alcoholism began to catch up with him.

> I started having uncontrollable outbursts and punched an officer and was court-martialed. I wasn't diagnosed with anything yet. But that's when my alcoholism really took its toll. . . . They put me into a substance abuse class at the same time I was in court-martial procedures, so I just stopped showing up for duty. I wouldn't show up for work anymore. . . . I finally got court-martialed and sent to the brig at Camp Lejeune.

FROM SOLIDER TO PRISONER: "IT'S ACTUALLY WORSE THAN CIVILIAN PRISONS"

Throughout this chapter we have seen how race and a lack of interconnected forms of institutional capital—having to tolerate overt racism in the line of duty (e.g., Vietnam era veterans), being disproportionately subjected to monotonous work, having to an endure a culture of masculinity that is characterized by a steely silence (e.g., "sucking it up")—create cumulative social deficits in the lives of some African-American veterans. Coupled with a lack of access to mental health service and substance abuse treatment, such respondents plunge deeper into the harsh and unforgiving military response to insubordination. It is therefore important to place some special emphasis on jarringly negative *within*-service turning points in the lives of black veterans, including incarceration (e.g., brig time). My dialogues with African Americans who did time in the brig begins with Terrence.

Interviewer: Tell me about being locked in the brig.

Terrence: I was stripped down and put on the row, disciplinary row. That means you are stripped butt naked and placed in your cell, locked down all day by yourself. There was nothing in there but a toilet. Over my five months in the brig, I was put in there like three or four times, because I wouldn't salute the captain. I told them, "Why should I salute you, when I'm going to be getting out of here in five months? There is nothing that you can do to me." So they took all my cigarettes, my toiletries, everything away from me.

Interviewer: Who was in there with you? Was it primarily African-American marines?

Terrence: Well, I was locked down on the row most of the time, so I didn't have much contact with anybody. But when I was able to see, it was just like the prisons I've been locked up in on the outside since after the military. The brig is nearly all black. This place was a hardcore penal institution; it's actually worse than civilian prisons. I mean at least when you get locked up on the outside most places you get access to medical and substance abuse treatment. In there, I was going through alcohol withdrawals and everything, because there's nothing in there. So by the end of this, I had no faith or trust in the Marine Corps anymore.

Interviewer: How did it end for you?

Terrence: I got a bad conduct discharge and they forcibly removed me from the base.

"IT WAS THE LONGEST THIRTY DAYS I HAD EVER SPENT IN MY LIFE"

Stephen, a young marine, introduced in the previous chapter, was also court-martialed and served time in the brig. His service began in Okinawa. After two years, Stephen's unit was deployed to a combat theater in East Timor, Indonesia. Soon thereafter Stephen was sanctioned for an alcohol violation. Despite this challenging situation, Stephen put in for an extension to stay in Okinawa but was denied and sent to the Camp Lejeune, North Carolina.

Interviewer: What was it like going to Camp Lejeune?

Stephen: I was devastated when they denied my extension in Okinawa. And I knew it was likely going to be difficult for me back on Lejeune.

Interviewer: Why?

Stephen: The same sergeant who gave me grief for the alcohol violation told me straight to my face, "I know some people in that unit you're going to, and I'm gonna call them before you get there and tell them about the shit bird marine they're getting." So, I felt this negative stigma was already on me when I got to Camp Lejeune.

In addition to the challenging circumstances that accompanied Stephen to Camp Lejeune, soon after his arrival he suffered a major personal tragedy in his life.

Interviewer: So that must have created a really difficult situation for you?

Stephen: Yeah, and shortly after I got there, my great-grandmother had passed away. She had complications from diabetes—got all kinds of infections—and then passed. So, I requested leave to be with my family. Because she was like a second grandmother to me. But in the regulations it doesn't allow for leave for great-grandmothers, only grandmothers, mothers, and what have you. But I was devastated and finally they gave me two days, so I go to the funeral. But that wasn't enough time to grieve. You know, by the time I was 7 years old, I spent my summers with her,

> so this wasn't cool. It was that combined with everything else going on. But I don't think I saw it then, I was just at a point where I stopped caring. I still tried to do what's right, but I felt tired a lot and very nonchalant, but I didn't know how to verbalize it.

Stephen, in effect, had to swallow his emotions and quickly return to duty.

Interviewer: That is a lot to deal with. . . . What happened?

Stephen: I just started drinking real hard. It just started getting worse and worse. I started to be late for duty and got an NJP [Non-Judicial Punishment] and they took rank for me. I guess I was fulfilling this whole "shit bird marine" idea that was in my head. So, I was real depressed by that.

In the absence of mental health treatment, Stephen was permitted to see a marine chaplain.

Interviewer: Did they offer any help?

Stephen: I was able to go see the chaplain. And you know I was brought up with a strict Christian upbringing, so I thought this could help. But I didn't feel any connection with him at all. So, the next time they asked me if I wanted to see him [the chaplain] again I said, "No." So by that point, the staff sergeant in charge said, "If you're late anymore or any more screw ups, you're getting NJP'd again." So, no, I was in the weeds. One more screwup and I could face court-martial, be dishonorably discharged. I mean they done take all my rank away by that point, so it got real serious.

Here, Stephen explains in excruciating detail the emotional turmoil he was suffering. Indeed, his depression becomes so bad that he describes himself experiencing suicidal thoughts.

> I felt so much pressure on me and my depression got worse and worse. . . . I was at a point in my life when I felt like everything good I had tried to do in my life was falling apart and that all that was left was what I had done wrong. And that's where the spotlight was. . . . So one night I went out and got drunk because of my depression. And I woke the next morning on the kitchen floor drunk and passed out. I looked at my watch and it was like nine o'clock, so I just busted out crying, because I knew that was it. I got nothing left. . . . I was feeling suicidal and so ashamed of myself that I didn't want to face the music. So I didn't go back to work. I couldn't go back. So one day became a lot of

> days. I had a total nervous breakdown. And then I went out and got drunk again to take my mind off of things, so before I knew it I had been gone for a week.

At this point, Stephen was utterly isolated from the world around him. Indeed, he barely made contact with his mother, someone he described in the previous chapter as maintaining a very close relationship with him.

Interviewer: Did you communicate at all with your family?

Stephen: Not really. I mean I called my mom once during this time just to let her know I was okay, that I was eating. But I didn't tell her where I was, because I knew if my sergeant contacted her she's a too honest of a woman, so she'd definitely tell him. So, she didn't know anything that was going on.

Finally, a girlfriend convinces Stephen to confront his superiors.

Interviewer: So when did you finally go back to duty?

Stephen: I went back just after two months. I attribute that to a woman I was seeing at the time. She was the only one supporting me, and she said, "You have to go back and face this, you can't just let this sit like this. If you want any future at all you gotta deal with this." So I said, "I know it, you're right, you're one hundred percent right."

Interviewer: What happened?

Stephen: She gave me the money for a cab and then I went back to platoon headquarters. And when he saw me and was like had this look on his face of like, "What the hell are you doing here, I've never been in a situation like this." So he said, "Have a seat and don't move." So I was like, "Yes, Staff Sergeant." I stayed overnight at headquarters. And then the next day, they started questioning me, "What's wrong with you?" "Are you okay, what the hell is wrong with you?" So they put me on restriction, because I was a flight risk for about two weeks. Then they informed that I was going to have a summary court-martial. I actually got off light. No dishonorable discharge or anything like that. And it was because I came back voluntarily. . . . I was lucky I did. . . .

Interviewer: What sanctions did you receive?

Stephen: Loss of rank, pay, and thirty days in the brig.

Interviewer: What was the brig like?

Stephen: You can't move from one place to another without a door locking behind you. It's total lock down. Let's just put it this way: it was the longest thirty days I had ever spent in my life. But I was model prisoner, never did anytime in the hole. Never had any fights or problems with anyone. But it tears you down, man. You know, you're a marine and now you are nothing. You're barely human in their eyes. But I just kept my head down and sucked it up.

"THEY PUT ME IN THERE FOR FOUR MONTHS"

The young Iraq War veteran, Andre, began a downward spiral that began during his nine and a half month tour. His story is particularly disturbing, especially considering all he had overcome to become a marine, including a childhood in Alabama filled with low education expectations from a white teacher and a debilitating foot injury that he had managed to overcome. Although training at Paris Island is challenging for any new recruit, Andre describes his experience as "excellent, I stayed in the top of my class. When I graduated boot camp, I felt on top of the world." With literally not a moment to rest, Andre was deployed immediately to the Middle East after boot camp.

Interviewer: What was it like when you got in country?

Andre: Kuwait was so hot. . . . I got off of the airplane. I had just took my last sip of American Sprite that I was gonna take for nine and a half months. I walk out and I take two steps and I have cottonmouth already; it feels like the sun is about to kiss me in the mouth. And it's at night, I thought I was gonna die there, I was like if a bullet don't kill me, the heat will. I mean it gets up to 125 [degrees] in the daytime and then at night you're looking at thirteen degrees. It's crazy in the desert."

Andre's unit only stayed in Kuwait for a short time. Within a week he arrived in Iraq and was stationed in Al Taqaddum, a base only a few miles from the dangerous city of Fallujah.

Interviewer: What was your job over there?

Andre: Well, we did security and my secondary specialty was supply, so when it comes to vehicles, gear, ammunition, we're on top of all that stuff. But my main job out there was

> working in a security force. We set up a man LPOP [Listening Post Observation Post], which is basically an observation post, and then we're responsible for either guiding or going outside the wire to assist, also we were responsible for quick reaction force. It was intense.

Andre next described the racial dynamics in his unit:

> In our security force? It was pretty much all black. But the thing is, the black marines that stood beside me out there were extremely well trained. Our commanding officers were white, but I had no problem with them until the bullets started flying. When the bullets started flying they'd always move behind us. Why would they do that? It pissed us off, but we just did our job. But I tell you what; they put us all in danger moving around like that.

Interviewer: What was the most blatant racist experience you encountered over there?

Andre: The most blatant racist thing to me was all black guys being ordered to actually go look for mines. I mean if we find one we're dead: so we never found any! [laughs]

Miraculously, no one in Andre's unit was killed in action:

> We did have some guys get wounded, but no casualties. And I think it really was the fact that all the black soldiers and the few Mexican Latino soldiers I served with were very sharp. We knew what we were doing out there. I mean you never leave a man behind, but you have certain tactics where if a soldier gets wounded you supposed to leave 'em out there for a minute because of sniper fire. But our reaction time on a down marine was so fast that we didn't lose anybody. . . . As soon as someone was hit, we got 'em and we taking 'em to the back. I know especially us minorities who were out in front—we took our training more seriously—we felt like any white soldier would let us die, rather than risk their lives for us. In fact, it happened, any time someone was left waiting out there, just sitting there bleeding, it's because the white first sergeants and officers had to run back and get us to pick them up. Maybe, they were scared to come get us!? [laughs] But it was bullshit and got worse as things dragged on.

Andre described himself as a leader in his unit. However, like many other respondents, he also describes a hostile climate that made it very hard to manage his emotions. Indeed, Andre was initially only supposed to serve in Iraq for seven months, but a white officer he describes as "out to get me" kept him in country for nine and a half months. For him, this situation was especially difficult to reflect upon.

Interviewer: Tell me about when you were told that you were going to have to stay two and a half more months in Iraq.

Andre: Oh man. . . . It was brutal, dog. . . . I mean I've got all the gear ready to go and then I'm ordered back and told that they needed me. Well, nothing changed, they were constantly ordering us to the front. And this one time—I mean I should have been home by now—we come under heavy mortar fire and were almost killed. Killed, for what?!? Killed because I think they wanted me to die. I honestly believe that's why they kept me there two and a half more months.

Interviewer: Did you still have to look for mines?

Andre: Oh yeah, more than ever. I mean it's ridiculous when you tell us to get off a truck and go look for them; they are on the road but obviously if we find one we're dead, 'cause they're gonna blow it up right there. But I was real fortunate.

Andre described feeling betrayed for having to stay an extra two and a half months in an exceptionally perilous combat arena. He described his white superior officers as "trying to kill me. . . . It's like hold on, hold on I'm not sitting here watching no regular post, know what I'm saying, we fighting to stay alive out here, know what I'm saying? But you gonna ask me what do I plan on doing when I go home? And then you turn around and gonna tell me I've gotta do two and a half more months? It's some kind of game or some kind of joke."

Once Andre finished his extended tour of duty in Iraq, he returned home to Camp Lejeune. Andre describes his return as an extremely hostile experience. His commanding officer imposed extremely strict rules on his leave time.

Interviewer: So what happened when you got home?

Andre: I took off. I went home to chill out. And then when I got back they put me on restricted duty for desertion.

Interviewer: Could you see your family again?

Andre: Yeah, but they told me they had some kind of new thing in the Marine Corps that because I was on restricted duty I had to call in every so often and let them know how I was doing. I was on their list. So, I took a two-week leave and called in. But what they didn't tell me was I had already used up most of my two weeks when I deserted. It was a setup. I mean I made my calls and everything and they never once told me about this. But guess what? When I got back I was given an NJP [Non Judicial Punishment]. I had gotten them before, but this time it was with the first sergeant and I knew the guy was racist. And he comes around me and smiling and putting his arm around me and asking me how my leave was then asks me am I ready to get another NJP. Soon as I find out what they was trying to NJP me for, I took myself to the library on base, I looked up my call records on my call logs, and I printed them out on a piece of paper. I went in there, I saluted the colonel, he talked about me like a dog, like I couldn't do nothing right. . . . So I just handed the call logs to him right there. And I told him, "I'm ready to do something with the rest of my life, if we can just end this."

Interviewer: So what happened?

Andre: They took me in and court-martialed me. They broke me all the way down to a private and locked me in the brig.

Interviewer: Oh no. . . . Can you tell me about that experience?

Andre: I mean I didn't feel like it was justice, you know what I'm saying? All I wanted to do was move on with my life, I didn't feel like this is what I needed to be doing anymore. I served y'all faithfully. I saved a lot of y'all lives, and now you gonna put me in here with murderers, rapists. They put me in there for four months in a very hot cell in isolation. I got no clothes. I can't even shower every day. I get less food than everyone else. They eat three times; I eat twice. Then they put me in population, and when I get out they nail me. I don't get dishonorable, but I get a bad conduct discharge that means y'all aren't ever gonna help me.

Rather than actively seek meaningful help for veterans such as Terrence, Stephen, and Andre, the military establishment allowed them to suffer in a brutal, torturous silence. There is no indication that any of these men received any meaningful interventions, even after they exhibited clear signs of depression, substance abuse, and emotional turmoil. To the contrary, they were each pushed to their collective breaking points. Terrence's story is particularly distressing. As a profoundly marginalized African-American man with an incredibly difficult upbringing—indeed, the kind of erratic behavior he describes seems part of his own cumulative struggles with poverty, mental illness, and substance abuse over the course of his life—and yet the military seemingly ignores even the most obvious of warning signs. Instead, while in a substance abuse class, Terrence is court-martialed and thrown into the brutal confines of the brig's disciplinary row. While the experiences of each is negative in the extreme, they serve as a useful segue into the unforgiving world of veteran's post-military experiences, a topic I explore in considerable detail in the book's next chapter.

Chapter Five

The Journey Home

Mel: These huge race riots broke out all around us. I remember when I saw the National Guardsmen came in and that's when I really started having problems. I was over at my buddy's house and just happened to look out the window and I said, "Oh shit, an army truck, and I saw another and another. And I was like, "What the hell is going on. We're being invaded!"

Carl: Yes, for a time I had to. It was survival. You know, am I going hungry tonight or not? That was a question I've asked myself too many times. But it was pretty widespread in Jersey. I mean things were going way downhill and people were getting locked up by the cops all over the place. I know, because I got some crazy twenty-year sentence for possession, but thankfully that was thrown out.

Andre: We can't get no job, so we out here surviving. But I'm starting to think there's nothing out here for us. In this white society, I either got to carry a microphone, a bottle, or a gun. Soldier, a rapper, or entertainer. Or playing some kind of sport or a boxer or a fighter or something. But it's not gonna happen. I mean so many of us don't have jobs or are in the street. . . . And don't even get me started on . . . credit card bills. . . . And we ain't even talking about eating. I know what it's like to be a veteran and have nothing to eat, you know what I'm saying?

When Carl returned home from Vietnam, he moved back to the small rural town of his youth. Like many Vietnam era vets who served in the late 1960s, his town had gone through dramatic changes. While Jim Crow segregation was still strictly enforced, African Americans in the community began to engage in acts of open-resistance to white supremacy. While Carl describes his return to civilian society as a "major struggle," he also recalls the intensifying movement for civil rights as "exciting . . . I made it home alive to be a part of some major stuff going on. I mean, when I left for the service blacks were forced to come into a restaurant from the rear entrance. We pretty much kept to our own and traveled in the shadows. But groups of people on the black part of town started to openly defy that. And you got to remember that this is a little town where voices travel far and everyone knows everyone and what not. But you got blacks of all ages marching together wanting to tear down those walls. It was surreal. I mean *surreal* is the only way I can describe that time."

I asked Carl how, if at all, black veterans were involved:

> Well, you know for us coming home from Vietnam it was all pretty intense. Plus, even in this small town there was a number of guys who were walking wounded in the black community, just walking around town in a daze. And we also had people that lost limbs. So it was hard for a lot of vets to really get involved. I mean, I wasn't maimed, and I personally thought it wasn't a good idea not to share or talk about the war with anybody. But you asked me about black people after I got home. . . . Hmmm. . . . I was really shocked to see black police officers! We now had people I knew as the police in our section of town. I mean, there were only two or three of them, but I knew one of them well—a friend's father who served in Korea.

I asked Carl what his relationship was like with this black officer and the others:

> They were great because with them around us we didn't see any white cops around—I don't have too many good memories of them before I left [laughs]—I mean, I actually can't remember any serious incident when a black officer arrested anyone. And it made sense that [father's name] was part of this new group of black police, because he was a man of honor, extremely proud of his service in Korea and now as a police officer. But I'd lie if I said it wasn't strange seeing a black man with a badge [laughs]! It just wasn't happening in our little Podunk town before I went into the service.

Set against a backdrop of major societal upheaval during the civil rights movement, four primary conditions seem critical for understanding the challenges African-American veterans face after returning home from service: a lack of steady employment and poverty, entanglements in the criminal justice system, health care marginality and the challenges of negotiating the VA, and the pervasive struggle to maintain strong social networks. Below I will draw on Carl's experience to illustrate each of these in turn. But as will become clear, how veterans experience each of these conditions is highly contingent upon the social context and the broader historical moment. In presenting each respondents' post-military stories, I will highlight various aspects of the four main characteristics presented below. This will entail a focus on a number of congruous themes that I believe best capture the particulars of the respondents' lived experiences at various points in their journeys home.

A LACK OF STEADY EMPLOYMENT AND POVERTY

Only months after he returned home, Carl was offered his old factory job back but decided that he had enough of small town life. He also had gotten married and became a father and "wanted my son to see the world beyond where I grew up." Eventually Carl was able to find a job as a day laborer in New Jersey. However, as the exchange below illustrates, maintaining a steady income was challenging for Carl.

Interviewer: Tell me about the challenges you faced trying to find employment.

Carl: I mean, it was a struggle. Jobs for day laborers were hard to come by, especially if the weather was bad: there was no work. And no work, meant no money, but I was able to draw my unemployment and keep my head above water.

During this time, Carl's sleep began to suffer from what he would much later learn was PTSD. Carl explained his own experience trying to find help for an ailment that at this time in history was not officially recognized. Moreover, Carl explains how unemployment, PTSD, and self-medication undermined his ability to be a reliable husband and father:

> I should have found counseling. But that's not what happened. I mean, the words "help for vets" wasn't on billboards, especially in the black community in New Jersey. I mean, I was dealing with so much that I completely lost touch with being a husband and a father. . . . I tried to be supportive. . . . I know that I could have had a better influence on my son's formative years if I had been living a different way. And I think that there was a price to be paid for that in the way he turned out—he's locked up for drugs now—because when he was growing up, I really started to drop out his life and everything around me. . . . And he always wanted to spend time with me. When I used to go out, he wanted to go with me. But I literally couldn't be there for him, because I wasn't there for myself. Again, I'm not making excuses, but that crazy war wouldn't let go of me.

Carl and his wife eventually separated and his work situation completely deteriorated, his addiction deepened, and he eventually became infected with HIV:

> I got deep into the lifestyle and was sharing needles. I'm not sure when it happened but I actually got infected with HIV, so I'm dealing with all those medications today. And also smoking crack. I mean, the black community in New Jersey started to change immensely, especially when crack hit. The temptation to make easy money was also huge.

Interviewer: Were you selling drugs?

Carl: Yes, for a time I had to. It was survival. You know, am I going hungry tonight or not? That was a question I've asked myself too many times. But it was pretty widespread in Jersey. I mean things were going way downhill and people were getting locked up by the cops all over the place. I know, because I got some crazy twenty-year sentence for possession, but thankfully that was thrown out.

The challenges of unemployment and poverty in a traumatized veteran's life led to aggressive self-medication, addiction, and HIV infection. Carl's life is characterized by a struggle to literally survive from one day to the next. He also alludes to being ensnared by the drug war. This circumstance, as will be illustrated in the next section, becomes especially pervasive in Carl's and his son's lives.

ENTANGLEMENTS IN THE CRIMINAL JUSTICE SYSTEM

Carl spends the next twenty years cycling in and out of the prison system on various drug charges. However, most of the time he does in prison is a series of short bids. In contrast, his son's drug-related activity results in a downward trajectory into the carceral system that results in far harsher consequences.

Interviewer: Did you do any other time in prison?

Carl: Oh yeah, I did some short bids for possession. But my son got hit much harder. By sixteen he had one brush with law enforcement. By the time he was eighteen, he was actually sent to a boot camp program. He's thirty-six now, and he's only been out a couple years in between that. He was locked up for a big chunk of his adult life; from age 22–31

> he was behind bars for selling crack. He finally got out and a little less than two years later he got busted again and got another ten years which he is doing now.

Other African-American veterans are able to altogether avoid the criminal justice system. Some are wrongfully convicted and subsequently exonerated. Still several others follow a trajectory similar to Carl's. From prison, they journey to halfway houses, long-term care in VA hospitals, or living a sizable chunk of their lives on the streets.

THE STRUGGLE TO MAINTAIN SOCIAL NETWORKS

Carl's own struggles with PTSD bled into his entire life. His social network eroded and catalyzed his struggles with addiction and serious health problems such as HIV. Compounding his health problems are the resultant broken bonds between Carl and his son. To learn more about his family situation, I was able to conduct a detailed interview with Carl's ex-wife, Pauline. Despite his long history as a profoundly marginalized African-American man, Pauline maintains a friendship with Carl. In the following exchange, it is also clear how his ex-wife went to Herculean lengths to get him into VA care.

Interviewer: Had it become clear to you early on into your marriage that Carl was suffering the effects of the war?

Pauline: Absolutely, it became apparent to me early on. . . . He had nightmares and heavy drinking and quickly drugs were involved. . . . It wasn't good, let's just put it that way.

Pauline also explains her reason to stay in touch with Carl is her dogged commitment to her son and family.

Interviewer: What made you stick by him all these years even after your divorce?

Pauline: Well, I gave birth to my son, I lost a daughter prior to having my son, and I believed I was in the fifth month of pregnancy, so I had a miscarriage. And it wasn't long after that that I became pregnant with my son. So I had a son, and my parents, they stayed together, and that's the way I grew up. I grew up in a family, and I wanted it that way. And I took a while. I would think, "How would I get through this?" I just couldn't understand why he was falling apart and couldn't get help.

Interviewer: And in the early '70s, people really didn't know how to care for Vietnam veterans.

Pauline: Right, he would be okay for five or six months. . . . Everything's okay and then all of a sudden, you know, I don't even know this person. I regretted that I stayed as long as I did.

Interviewer: How long were you married?

Pauline: Oh goodness, I think we got married in '72 and I left in '86 I believe.

Interviewer: Tell me about your son. . . . It must have been challenging raising him on your own.

Pauline: When I left my husband I think my son was about 12 years old. But he had already seen so much. . . . Carl was not a good father. So my son grew up seeing things he shouldn't have seen as far as drugs and what not. And . . . I don't know. . . . He ended up with issues of his own.

Interviewer: When did you then start to talk to Carl again?

Pauline: Not long after our divorce. I was always hoping that he would do better for himself. And he went into programs and got out. And I guess he tried to be a better person or make amends for some of the things he did in the past. And he always called, and I would check on him to see if he was okay.

Interviewer: What has been the most challenging part of that process?

Pauline: Carl will just disappear. He won't call or he won't pick up the phone when you call to check on him. He won't answer. It seems like he goes into these depressions, I don't know.

Interviewer: But you've still managed to maintain a friendship?

Pauline: I do, yes. I consider him a friend.

At the time of our interview in 2009, Pauline remained a vital part of Carl's social network. Not only had he maintained a friendship with her by phone, but she has come to his aid several times in the years after their divorce.

Interview: So, when things are in crisis, you are still one of his main go-to people?

Pauline: Mm hmm. I drove from Florida to Ohio to get him out of a situation several years ago. I was so scared. He was living with, I don't know who these people were, but I think they

> were drug involved. He would stay there, and at the end of the month he would owe them his money. And he acted like, he said he couldn't get away. So, I said, "When you get your VA check get a bus ticket, and just get on the bus and go. Just leave!" He couldn't seem to be able to do it. So I got in my car, I talked to my current husband. I said listen, "Carl's in Ohio and he can't seem to get away. He needs to be in a hospital somewhere and he's staying with someone that I guess from month to month is on drugs." So, I said, "I am going to go get him to the VA hospital in Maryland." So I drove to Cleveland and back. I took him to the hospital in Maryland and then drove back to Florida.

HEALTH CARE MARGINALITY AND THE CHALLENGES OF THE VA

Carl confirms that, in his words: "I'd be dead if weren't for Pauline. There's no doubt about it. She's always been there for me." I asked Carl if he had other friends or supportive allies. In contrast to some of the veterans I interviewed, Carl describes his relationship in recent years with VA counselors and doctors as very strong. As Pauline confirms, "Carl has been blessed with the VA. Because everything that he ever has a problem with they take him in. And they encourage him to come back—his doctors stay in touch with him—even to the point of just checking on him."

For Carl, the VA is the organization that provides the single most important form of support. It is a literal lifeline for him, as he suffers from serious ailments and is dependent on disability benefits and the long-term care in VA hospitals such as Coatesville, Pennsylvania. But for many black veterans who return to racially aggrieved communities and must negotiate entanglements with unemployment, housing inequality, family crises, and, indeed, their own serious health conditions, navigating the VA's notoriously complex bureaucracy becomes too overwhelming. As we will learn, obtaining support from the VA often requires incredible persistence. Black veterans must be relentless in their pursuit of benefits. Indeed, for Vietnam era veterans like Carl and others, VA centers did not recognize combat related trauma (e.g., PTSD) until several years after their return, and the lack of accessibility has been devastating. As Carl observes: "I mean, for years after I got back there weren't any vet centers that I knew of. I think the closest one was six hours away in Virginia. It was actually more than *ten years* after getting back from Vietnam before I set foot inside a vet center."

Even after his first visit, following up on appointments was extremely difficult. For one, he lived in a spatially isolated place, lacked steady employment, and was criminalized for petty drug use that led to serious health problems, including HIV-infection. The legacy of the Vietnam War took a serious toll on an impoverished black man and his family, and in the absence of meaningful, sustained health care he was, for many years, left literally to fend for himself. As Carl explains, "I knew I had some problems. I just wasn't, I couldn't pinpoint, or I didn't really pursue it or address it properly. . . . I was always hoping that when I got back here to the States I could take up and forget about it, that wasn't to be. And I did survive obviously the Vietnam experience, but before I knew dealing with normal life was one crisis after another."

A turning point in Carl's life began after he filed a claim with the VA. To be sure, his was a long struggle. Fortunately, the Disabled American Veterans (DAV) were able to assist him with negotiating the VA's cumbersome bureaucracy. Even with the help of the DVA, Carl describes the process of receiving disability benefits as a dramatic struggle:

> At first I didn't trust them. I had heard from other brothers that they just made you wait and treated you like a piece of meat. And some of the VAs I've been to was like that. But I've been lucky overall as I've gotten a lot of great care. A lot of the credit goes to the DVA. They got a lot of information together for me and it forced the VA's hand. But I had to continuously find a way to physically get to the VA! In a strange way, getting real sick was a blessing in disguise. Because I could stop chasing them. I made sure things were being processed through my various counselors and I was finally awarded 100 percent disability. It wasn't so much for the money, although I was broke and if I wasn't in the VA hospital, I was living on the street. So it definitely helped [laughs], but I really just wanted them to acknowledge what this war did to people, because I knew it was not just me, but a lot of other vets.

I asked Carl what his experience has taught him about the challenges facing today's generation of black veterans:

> You gotta be prepared to push on. This will be a long fight, because just like the way the black community has been treated—I mean look at my son—locked up for most of his life—you're not going to get a hand from anyone. Only other veterans can help you. And now that I'm not living on the street anymore and am here at Independence House, I've made it my mission to reach out to other younger black vets to encourage them to go to the VA and get what's coming to them. I want to spend the rest of my life trying to have some influence there to make a difference. I mean, a lot of the young guys coming back from Iraq and Afghanistan are just getting on the path that nearly killed me. But I came down it, and I hope that my experience will mean

something more to them so when I try to help them or offer some advice they listen, not because someone told them how it could be, but because they're hearing it from someone who has lived it.

MEL: "THESE HUGE RACE RIOTS BROKE OUT ALL AROUND US"

Recall from the previous chapter that Mel returned home from Vietnam on Christmas Eve of 1967. In contrast to Carl, he moved back into a setting with a large and supportive network of family and friends. Mel's journey home, however, cannot in any way be characterized as an "easy" one. But it is clear that both strong support from his family and steady employment enabled him to transition back into civilian society in a way that is markedly different from most other marginalized African-American veterans that I interviewed. Whereas Carl's weak social networks, lack of steady employment and attendant poverty, health problems, entanglements with the criminal justice system, and struggles with the VA created enormous challenges in his journey home, Mel recalls his biggest challenges began *in* the community. In contrast to Carl's ability to keep a low profile in a small rural town in the crucible of the civil rights movement, Mel's experience in a comparatively large urban community presented different challenges:

Interviewer: How were you treated after Dr. King's assassination?

Mel: I mean I wasn't called baby killer or anything like that, but black people in my community couldn't even look me in the eye, even people that once were my friends don't want anything to do with me. They couldn't understand why a black man was in Vietnam when we don't have our rights here. And that hurt me, but I got so mad I just I basically shut off from the outside world and stayed to myself.

Soon after his return, Mel also felt some estrangement from his parents. As the following exchange illuminates:

Interviewer: How was your family when you first moved home after the war?

Mel: It was weird at home too. I remember my younger brothers couldn't have toy guns and nothing like that, and I might be watching something on TV about war or something like that and my mother would actually come in and turn the channel! "What the hell is wrong with these crazies?" I'm thinking something's wrong with them, but they were basically trying to safeguard me from certain things, then that get to the point when you want to say, "Whoa, wait a minute, please stop."

Approximately six months after his return home, Mel had his first of several bouts of reoccurring malaria and was hospitalized with intense fevers and violent body tremors. As he described this harrowing experience, he also was quick to note that his family provided invaluable support: "I was lucky because the whole family was always there for me and around my hospital bed." In addition to his health problems, Mel was amazed at how dramatically his neighborhood would change that summer after the assassination of Dr. King.

Interviewer: Do you remember what was happening in the city at this time?

Mel: These huge race riots broke out all around us. I remember when I saw the National Guardsmen came in and that's when I really started having problems. I was over at my buddy's house and just happened to look out the window and I said, "Oh shit, an army truck, and I saw another and another. And I was like "What the hell is going on, we're being invaded!"

Next, Mel describes a stunning confrontation with a National Guardsman:

> So me and buddy got in my car and started hauling ass home, and this National Guardsman jumped in front of me, and said, "Stop, you can't go down there. So, I got out of my car and I said, "I live right down there." And he says, "I don't care, you can't go there." I don't remember what happened next, but the next thing I know I have his rifle in my hands; I took it from him. My buddy's in the car hollering, "Mel, please give it back to him, give it back to him," and I'm saying, "No! I just got back from 'Nam and this damn toy soldier's gonna tell me I can't go home, who the fuck does he think he is?!" But then my mind clicked in and was like "Are you stupid?!" So I handed his rifle back to him and within like seconds the cops are all over me. But fortunately one of the cops recognized me and knew I just got back from 'Nam, so he told this National Guardsman that everything was alright, that I did, in fact, live over there, and they let me go.

As the riots escalated, Mel describes himself and other black veterans confronting the ringleaders who he described as "Tearing up our neighborhood. I mean they destroyed the liquor store, grocery store, and we vets were like, 'Whoa, ya'll make no sense.' So we had a meeting with them and we tried to organize them into teams—like in 'Nam—to take back parts of the city that were occupied with the main goal to take over city hall. But they thought we were crazy, so our meeting went nowhere. These fools wanted to play games and burn down their own house, burn down their own stores, that's gonna help them out—burning everything that's theirs but don't go where you supposed to go?"

"WHEN WE FIRST WENT TO THE VA THEY TREATED US HORRIBLY"

Any engagement Mel had with the struggle for racial justice in the streets soon gave way to his own struggles with post-combat related trauma. Beyond the erroneous story of the "confused" or "bewildered" Vietnam veteran powerfully critiqued in the work of sociologist Jerry Lembcke,[1] Mel's struggles are more clearly understood in a broader social context. Perhaps most clearly, the traumatized veteran's experience is intensified when one considers the aggressive backlash against civil rights that was being waged against African Americans in their own communities at this time. A conflagration on the home front provokes outrage on the part of those black veterans who must confront a bureaucratic and unsympathetic VA. Mel describes his initial experience with the institution:

Interviewer: So tell me about your first experiences with the VA.

Mel: When we first went the VA treated us horribly. The way they talked to us: They said we were the crybabies. I mean the workers at the VA looked at us like they was doing us a damn favor. I mean, they were actually nasty. And so my struggle went on like this for ten fucking years! But I had a major chip on my shoulder, and I simply wasn't going to be denied.

Even after his first formal recognition of entitlement to some disability benefits, it took two more decades—indeed, a full thirty years—before Mel received *full* disability benefits from the VA. One clear indication of Mel's perseverance was his refusal to leave, even after he was asked by personnel. But, as Mel explained, he "was pretty good at softening them up." Indeed, sympathetic VA workers began assigning Mel tedious tasks.

Interviewer: Do you recall any particular experiences when this occurred?

Mel: The VA had pretty much closed for the night. The only two people on the floor were me and Dr. ——. I mean his secretary was gone and he happened to look at one of the reports I wrote, and he said "Mel did you write up this paperwork?" And I said, "Yeah, but I ain't no secretary. I

> been to enough psychiatrists that I know what they gonna ask and not ask and I know when to shut up and when not to shut up." And he asks me if I wanted to be a VA counselor. So I said yeah [laughs].

"TRY AND GET BLACK VETS TO COME TO THE VET CENTER"

One of Mel's main jobs was not, however, to do counseling at the VA. Instead, he was given a vehicle in order to recruit black vets to come to meetings, which Mel described as one of the most difficult jobs he ever had:

> You want to see the hardest thing in the world to do? Try and get black vets to come to the vet center! They knew what I wanted, and didn't want to interact with the VA's white folks for any reason whatsoever. . . . I mean, I didn't even have addresses. I would park the car and start canvassing street corners, because I knew where people hung out and stuff like that. I'd find 'em drinking and drink right along with them [laughs]! And then I'd tell them who I was, and I say out of sixty guys I met, I convinced maybe twenty to come to meetings. There was so much resistance.

Mel explains how he still encounters black veterans who have not pursued benefits through the VA:

> There was a guy about a year ago and we sit down and talking about the neighborhood or whatever, and I don't know how it came up, but I come to find out he served in 'Nam. I looked at him and said, "You what!?" And I find out this guy has literally never been to the VA. But he didn't even want to go there. He said he didn't want to be treated like a piece of meat and deal with the games you have to play. And I totally understand it. I was just too damn persistent for them [laughs]. And now with these young guys coming home from Iraq—actually one of my daughter's friends—he said he didn't want to deal with the VA, and I said, "Boy, you better get your ass down there!" And I just explained to him what to do and most of all to be persistent. You gonna get it eventually! I said, look at your file; you were injured and you're aching in pain. Take some medicine now—go to the emergency room, if you have to—because you're gonna get the money from the VA! I told him every year you put this off, it's another check in their pocket, so I'm staying on him.

Despite his commitment to his own numerous health struggles, Mel uses his own experiences to educate other black veterans he encounters in everyday life. It is sobering, however, to remember that in comparison to the vast majority of black veterans I interviewed, Mel lives in the "good" section of the city and is fully engaged in raising his grandson. Mel is thus no longer able to provide the kind of difficult outreach efforts that he was engaged in as an employee of the VA. On the other hand, it is also important to remember that Mel's own apartment is a tiny two bedroom unit in an aging complex that is on the very edge of the city's most marginalized neighborhoods. The precariousness of his living situation is critical for understanding why the struggle to survive is at the center of Mel's life today. Not only as a combat veteran of the Vietnam War, but as was presented in a previous chapter, as a grandfather now charged with the very challenging responsibility of raising his young grandson.

BOBBY: "I COULDN'T UNDERSTAND WHAT WAS GOING ON"

Being a parent can take many unexpected turns for veterans. For some, the experience can be very positive and simultaneously devastating. When I met Bobby in his room at IH, I wasn't sure what to expect. He had been through a lot and because I did not want him to relive painful memories, as the following section reveals, I almost had to end the interview. Bobby insisted we continue, and I'm grateful because I believe his interview provides important insight into how PTSD is very much interwoven into an amalgam of traumatic experiences in the lives of veterans of color.

For a combat veteran like Bobby who has long suffered with PTSD this involved knowledge about a child's victimization. As we will see, such revelations can trigger feelings of uncontrollable, if not, paralyzing rage. Bobby would not learn about his own daughter's traumatic experiences until many decades after his return from Vietnam. Although he is not nearly as forthcoming as other veterans I interviewed, Bobby's decision to talk about this relatively recent situation came shortly after he began describing his first memories of returning from Vietnam to civilian life.

When Bobby returned home in 1972, his home city of Philadelphia was not under siege. As an alternative to Mel, his experience was not of rioting and almost immediate alienation, but much more of sensory overload. Bobby describes literally hitting the ground when he heard a car tail pipe backfire. Or ducking for cover at that sound of a loud voice. For him this meant creating a strategy for surviving civilian life: What Bobby calls "living by the numbers":

> I couldn't understand what was going on because I was still living by the numbers. I get up at four in the morning, run, and eat breakfast. I alienated myself from people and my family. But they allowed me that space because they knew that I was going through something. Then I started coming out of my cocoon after about six months. Now people in my circle, that I went to school with in Philly, we'd be sitting around talking, drinking a beer, and one day a buddy of mine—also a vet—suggested that we should go to one of these

> programs for Vietnam vets. And we started going there, and we identified that we weren't the only ones going through this. But at the time they didn't have the title PTSD, they called it shell shock.

Here, without my prompting, Bobby describes to me a reoccurring nightmare that nearly pushed him to the brink:

> Like I said, every time I heard a loud noise I would jump. I couldn't sleep. I had reoccurring nightmares of the first time that I had shot somebody. [In the dream] I was scared to shoot back, but the adrenaline was there and it seemed like the whole war stopped and that person was shooting at me. So, now I gotta decide that if he comes running at me, am I gonna shoot him or is he gonna shoot me? And as soon as I looked up I pointed my weapon in his direction and pulled the trigger. He stays alive long enough, so I can see his face. And that face stayed with me for a long time.

"MY PTSD CAME BACK AFTER ALL THE WORK I HAD DONE"

Fortunately, for Bobby his involvement with Vietnam veteran groups was very therapeutic. He described it as "really exciting to me because I wasn't by myself, I got other brothers with me who went through these exact same things that I went through. I also started getting involved with a lot of organizations like the VFW and the DVA and so I was doing pretty well." At this point in the interview, I could tell that Bobby started to feel uncomfortable, so I offered to end it:

Interviewer: It sounds like something happened that was very uncomfortable. If you want to end the interview, I completely understand.

Bobby: No. . . . Well, I mean it's hard. Because we're talking many, many years after all of this. I had been home from the war for twenty-five years. I mean I got a family and things are going real well and we have a strong church life and things had been fine for a long time. And so this happens like five years ago in 2004: My daughter comes to me and says, "Dad I got something to tell you." I said, "What's that?" She said, "Many years ago, I got molested." And it was like— Bam!— I heard her, but I didn't hear her, you know what I'm saying? So I said, "Who molested you? Are you gonna tell me? You know who it is?" And she told me, and that was a bitter pill to swallow. My PTSD came back after all the work I had done. I had to get hospitalized because I had so much anger. I had anger for what he did to my baby. I had resented myself, because I wasn't the father I should've been. When I told my other daughter the whole story she asked me, "What good are you to your children, if you kill that guy and you go to jail for the rest of your life?" And I had forgot all about God and friends. All I was focused on was this person.

After Bobby returned from the hospital, he explains that he had to make a difficult decision:

> I realized I can't speak much to my daughter who had been molested. . . . In like five years, I've spoken very little to her. I just don't wanna deal with her in any capacity because she deprived me of knowing what happened. But she's married now, so I feel good because she trusts men again.

"I'M INNOCENT"

In terms of Bobby's own experience with homelessness, it seems clear that this was a new experience for him. While he has suffered with alcohol, he is very well-spoken and described a successful career running a construction company. In comparison to many other veterans I interviewed at IH, he seemed oddly out of place to me.

Interviewer: How did you wind up here at IH?

Bobby: Oh man, this is quite a story. Two years ago, I got a phone call from a friend. An old buddy from Vietnam. I hadn't spoken to him in many years. And he's like, "This is John." And I'm like, "The only John I know got his legs blown off in 'Nam. He said, "Yeah that's me." He said, "I need you to help me move." I said, "Man you must be joking, you ain't got no legs!" He said, "No, all I want you to do is drive a truck." So, anyway we moved him in, and then he gets a phone call and says, "Well, I got to go." And it was raining profusely that night like a shower head. So I started to cross the street to go to my truck and a light was shown on me and I heard a voice, "I am a state trooper. I wanna talk to you." So I said, "What the heck is going on?" And he said, "Stop, get down on one knee." And then I got locked up. Apparently, about a hundred yards down the road someone broke into a store. So, I'm sitting there and he says, "No problem, the owners are coming right now to identify you." So anyway the owner came and said, "That's not the man." I said, "Officer you heard what he said get these handcuffs off me." He said, "No, you going to jail, nigger." I said, "You son of a bitch."

After lengthy questioning, Bobby was informed by a detective that he believed that Bobby wasn't the suspect, but that the detective believed Bobby knew who was.

Bobby: I told him I don't know anything about it. And the investigator is like, "What, are you calling me a liar?" I said, "Well, you are a liar." So now I was ready to go ahead and get beat down by these state troopers. But anyway, he takes me to jail. And it takes them three months to tell me what I've done, because I wouldn't accept no plea bargain, which means admitting you're guilty. I'm innocent. So they find me a lawyer. Any way it turns out it was some sting gone wrong. And they let me go with a bunch of apologies: "I'm very sorry for incarcerating you for this period of time. Take this card to my lawyer and he'll know what to do." So I got a big thick list of apologies from the state trooper.

Although his exoneration was a relief, Bobby describes numerous unforeseen financial problems:

Bobby: All the sudden my VA check is cut down to nothing. So, I said, "Whoa, what's going on here?" And the VA said, "Cuz you a fugitive felon." I said this is a mistake. And sure enough, there was a mistake between transposing from the paperwork to the computer. . . . I'm still listed as guilty! So, I've got next to no money to live on. . . . And then I heard about IH from a VA outreach counselor and thought, "Well, this is the only option I got."

"WE ALWAYS PRAY FOR EACH OTHER"

Fortunately, Bobby has a very close family as well as strong relationship with a VA psychiatrist he describes as "very important to me and always available whenever I need to talk." Bobby describes the important supportive role both religion and his siblings play in his present circumstances:

> My brother is always close to me. He also served in 'Nam. He has his own life and his own issues, but we share a very strong bond both spiritually and as veterans. I have an older sister who's an interior designer and my younger

sister who's a schoolteacher and another sister who's a homemaker. So they all have their own lives, but we always pray for each other. You know I'm still able to get up in the morning, still blessed, still shown favor from God. I love to pray for people and just sit back and watch God just work. So am I angry about this situation? Sometimes. Okay, but I know there's a reason for me to be going through this. I even ask God from time to time: "Lord what are you trying to tell me? You took my VA money and now I'm stuck here in Delaware. What are you trying to tell me?" So I'm waiting.

Interviewer: Have you heard from your daughter?

Bobby: I've called one and she gave me the whole picture of the whole family. You know she just loved to tell me everything. And right now you know they're protected. God's looking out for them. All my children are grown now. I don't worry about them, because I keep them in my prayers.

Bobby's journey home is a remarkable one. Unlike many other respondents, very soon after his return from Vietnam he is fully in his recovery from "shell shock." While the details of his engagement with the VA are unclear, his story of his daughter's molestation is a devastating example of how PTSD goes beyond the individual and may be triggered by traumatic events in civilian life, even many decades later. Bobby's entanglement with the criminal justice system and his subsequent plunge into homelessness is also profound—both as a critique of plea bargaining and as a guilty-plea system that is notoriously unjust and unreliable. And even after his exoneration, Bobby still must wait for his name to be officially cleared; a problem that has cut into his VA benefits and leaves him in a very precarious situation financially. In addition to the numerous social deficits in his journey home, Bobby's story also speaks to the power of family networks and religious faith in his life. Indeed, Bobby's prayer life provided important emotional capital throughout his combat service in Vietnam and into his present predicament.

EARL: "SHE THREW ME OUT OF THE HOUSE, AND I WOUND UP STAYING AT A SHELTER"

Earl returned home to a city that was hard hit by the race riots of previous years. Steady employment in Wilmington was very difficult to come by, so his only option was to move back into the projects with his mother. Similar to Lionel's experience, all the apartments were subjected to unannounced raids. For Earl, this was especially trying because as a 22-year-old veteran he was technically living there illegally. Fortunately, although he described the workplace as still a dead end for blacks, Earl was eventually able to get his old job with the power company (see chapter 4) back and moved out of his mother's apartment shortly thereafter. However, like other black Vietnam veterans I interviewed, stagnant wages and difficulties transitioning back into a civilian society leaves Earl "never feeling comfortable" on what will be an extraordinarily challenging journey home.

Interviewer: So how did things go after you moved out?

Earl: Well, I was glad to have moved out, but I just couldn't readjust to the job. Plus, I had taken to drinking in the military, and that was catching up with me.

Interviewer: You lost your job?

Earl: Yeah, lost the job at the power plant. And I also had gotten married and had a daughter, so things were real hard when the money was gone and my drinking continued. I had some scuffles with my wife. So she threw me out of the house, and I wound up staying at a shelter.

Interviewer: Did you contact the VA?

Earl: Well, it's interesting. Because it was there at that first shelter—I bummed a cigarette off of a guy—and he come to find out I was a veteran. And he said, "You got to go to the VA center. They got all kinds of programs there." I never knew about any of it. And I had some serious depression and I wound up in long-term care at Coatesville VA Hospital in Pennsylvania. And I met another vet there that I didn't get along with.

In a startling turn of events, Earl's first stay at Coatesville led to a completely unforeseen but horribly traumatizing experience in his life:

Earl: Make a long story short, I got into a fight at Coatesville and this guy pulled a knife on me. . . . And then, I'll never forget this, another vet I knew, broke it up. . . . So, I come to find out that this guy who pulled the knife on me—when he left the VA hospital—he murdered his wife and kids and killed himself. And I felt a lot of guilt for that. I mean if this guy had killed me, then he would've been locked up and never have gotten to his wife and kids. . . . That sent me on a drinking and drugging binge like none I've ever experienced before.

Earl lived on the streets for many months. Camping out in cemeteries, under bridges—indeed, wherever he "could stay hidden," Earl would go. Finally, after suffering a nervous breakdown, Earl checked himself into Coatesville's psychiatric ward, an experience he described as "a lot like prison, only crazier." It was at Coatesville where Earl learned that he was bipolar and that he was suffering from non-combat related PTSD probably as a result of the incident with the knife-wielding homicidal veteran he encountered in his first stay.

Interviewer: So how long were you able to stay at Coatesville?

Earl: It's only ninety days. So, since I've been out of the service, life has been a revolving door for me. In and out of halfway houses and thirty-day programs.

Interviewer: Were any of them effective?

Earl: There was one program I did that was for eighteen months in rural Pennsylvania—that was longest program I ever did—I got clean. And I got a job. I worked at a chicken factory, and I stayed there for four years and stayed clean for seven years. I got an apartment; I had my own place for the first time since I was married. But working at the factory was hard, man. And the pay wasn't good. And I ended up getting into a fight with my boss and lost my job. So, I picked up my check and couldn't find another job, so I started drinking again.

"I WANT TO BE ABLE TO GET SOME THINGS FOR HIM"

Earl soon returned to the streets in the most impoverished and racially aggrieved sections of Wilmington. While he had a brother in the area, he soon realized that his many months on the streets had created a difficult stigma for him to overcome:

Interviewer: You mentioned your brother, did you ever reach out to him for help?

Earl: I did once. My brother took me in. But his wife wouldn't accept me because she said I was a bum and I stunk. I was gonna take a bath and everything, but she wouldn't have it, so I left. And that was six years ago. But I ain't ever gone back, because I could see I caused friction between him and his wife, and I wasn't ever gonna let that happen again.

Earl describes that this experience convinced him to be very cautious with reconnecting with family in any especially direct ways. While he speaks with his siblings on the telephone from time to time, he's very wary of being seen for "fear of causing friction." However, Earl describes his daughter as incredibly supportive and simply unwilling to allow him to go too long without a visit:

Earl:	I have stayed the closest with her. She accepts me and wants me to stay at her house. But I've been homeless for so long now that just like with my brother, I don't want to cause friction. But I still stay in touch with her. She's a single mom, so at least it's just me and her and my grandson. Actually, about a week ago she had me over for dinner and asked me to stay over, but I said, "No."
Interviewer:	Did you get to spend time with your grandson?
Earl:	Oh yeah. And I love that. I talk to him. I really don't want him to have to go through what I've been through. I know it won't be easy, being a young black male living in the projects. I know it won't all be peaches and roses, but you don't have to be violent. You don't have to do drugs and drink like your grandfather. Or be miserable or be angry.
Interviewer:	Do you get to spend time together?
Earl:	Yeah, he's only 6 years old, so I've taken him to the park. I want to get him some things, but I don't have any money, so it's hard. My daughter actually caught me one day. She gave me some money for cigarettes, and I bought him a soda and chips with the money. And she said, "Dad, you don't have to do that." But I want to. I want to be able to get some things for him.

Both Carl (see chapter 2) and Earl describe similar longings to be the grandfathers they never could be, to confront longstanding housing inequalities, and to stay clean and sober. While Earl never saw combat in Vietnam, the war at home took a pervasive and heavy toll on him. In addition to the myriad of marginalities in his life, Earl's fist connection with the VA leads to an extraordinarily traumatic situation in which another veteran who previously tried to stab him returns home and murders his family. Earl feels profound guilt for this situation, wishing that "he killed me, so he wouldn't have gotten to the kids." Yet despite it all, Earl is able to stay connected with his daughter and grandson.

OTIS: "I FELT LIKE THERE WAS NOTHING I COULD DO"

Otis's description of his return to his old neighborhood paints a visceral portrait of urban black America in the Vietnam era. While his journey home to Wilmington in the early 70s began after the riots had simmered down, it is clear that many of the friends he grew up with were forever damaged by the war. Otis is then profoundly connected to the war at home as it plays out in the lives of other Vietnam veterans as well as his own challenges readjusting into civilian life. Even though he did not see direct combat in Vietnam, it is clear that a series of events with roots in his childhood are important for making sense of his post-war experience. For example, his continued connections decades later to childhood contacts profoundly impacted by the war, joblessness, poverty, and subsequent drug addiction steered Otis into a particularly dire time in his life. Moreover, Otis's own ability to be upwardly mobile in the years after his homecoming is also enmeshed in a broader social context. However, in contrast to most veterans, Otis's ability to attain advanced degrees led to nearly two decades of job stability. Although this employment experience ended on a personally devastating note for Otis in the context of his broader journey home, it helps to clarify his current struggles. We begin with a dialogue about the years just after his homecoming.

Interviewer: So you mentioned that you returned to your old neighborhood when you got back from Vietnam—tell me about how the war had impacted things at home.

Otis: It was very hostile, very bad. I couldn't believe what was happening. I mean, so many of my friends—neighbors who grew up right next door to me—had served in 'Nam. I didn't know, because I never saw any of them over there. But what struck me the most was how many of them served in combat and how bad things became for them. It was like a gut punch to see your peaceful neighborhood so divided and hopeless. Yeah, man, that's the word for it, hopelessness.

Interviewer: What do you most remember in terms of the change?

Otis: Everyone is so cut off from one another and my buddies had suffered so much. I remember one guy—a very nice guy—I went to school with him. But I guess when he went to Vietnam that experience really messed with his mind. He would show up on people's doorsteps begging for help, babbling uncontrollably. Everyone was scared of him. . . . And he actually ended up going off. . . . And the police shot

	him and killed him right in front of us. I mean, I went to Vietnam and was doing data processing and never saw a veteran killed until I got home! How messed up is that!? And there was another guy who lived two doors down from me, who I grew up with. Mentally, he was totally gone. It was bad. And that bothered me, because like I said I was fine compared to them, but I was hurting inside because I couldn't do anything for them.
Interviewer:	Did you try to take any of them to hospital or VA?
Otis:	No . . . I didn't know about the VA or what to do. There wasn't PTSD back then so, like I said, it was hopeless. I felt like there was nothing I could do for them. I mean they were living in the streets and their minds were gone. I ain't ever seen anything like it in Vietnam. So, no, I didn't know what could be done for them. I mean, these guys saw people killed over there and I'd probably been the same way.

Otis continues with broader reflections on the treatment of Vietnam veterans. He describes himself as still bitter about the way they were treated, and he believes that today's returning veterans have it much better off than his generation:

> I still have bitter feelings about the way Vietnam veterans were treated. I mean now is a good time to be an American veteran. But our generation, we were forgotten. I mean, Vietnam guys still today are jumping through hoops at the VA. I myself am struggling with depression and they make me jump through hoops. I know there are so many worse off than me who don't even try to go to the VA because they're too bitter. . . . I mean, the young guys are priority, and we're treated like a forgotten bunch of fools.

At the time of his return from Vietnam, Otis lived with his parents and sister. While he was able to begin to work and plan for the future, his father's drinking had become much worse. Recall from the previous chapter that Otis presumed his father's alcohol abuse was rooted in trauma he had suffered as a soldier in World War II. But after he returned from Vietnam, his father's drinking and subsequent rages became much less predictable. Not only would his father fly into drunken rages and punch his mother and sister, Otis's father tried to kill him only a few months after moving home:

> When I got home from Vietnam, my sister and her husband was living in my parents' house and then I moved in. And my sisters were very protective of me even when I got home. And my dad got into a tussle. He was throwing blows at my sister and I pushed him away. And then he went and got the shotgun and

> shot down the stairs at me. My brother-in-law grabbed it out of his hands, but my pops got a knife from some place and he come rushing down the stairs and went to stab me. But he didn't know I had a hammer and—smack!—I hit him in the head with the hammer a couple of times. I ain't proud of it [choked up]. I mean, the scar I put on his head was the last thing I saw on his face when he was lying dead in his casket [several years later].

"I LOST MY JOB AFTER NINETEEN AND A HALF YEARS"

Despite a dangerously volatile home with life marked by profoundly traumatic events for both Otis and his family, he persevered; eventually he moved out of his parents' house and took advantage of his GI Bill benefits. Otis went to small community college in the city. This enabled him to leave a low-paying mailroom job that he took soon after moving back in with his parents. Otis describes his decision to pursue an advanced degree:

Otis: When I was working in the mail room in this office building, I got to know some guys in collections and cost accounting and that intrigued me. I was dirt poor shuffling mail, so working with money seemed like something I could do. I loved numbers as a data processor, so I decided to pursue a business degree. Bad choice, looking back, because we know how the computer industry took off, but my mindset was to make better of the situation I was already in. I liked the company, but wanted to do more than mail room stuff. . . . So I got an associate's degree in business management and then a bachelor's in business administration. And then I got a job doing payroll for a bigger company.

Interviewer: Did you ever get married?

Otis: Oh yeah, I met my ex-wife in the late 80s. I had been working payroll for ten years and by then an old friend from the neighborhood introduced us. She came from the south—a real country girl—we were total opposites. But for some reason it worked out for like ten years. But losing that job was the worst thing that ever happened to me.

Interviewer: Yeah, it sounds devastating. . . .

Otis: It was devastating. We had bought a house and were living there for about five years and I lost my job after nineteen and a half years. They trumped up some charges against me, because this company would not let anyone get their twenty years. And I was devastated. I tried to file suit against them. But my lawyer told me I had no case, because they can fire you for anything. So I found myself standing in the unemployment line—it was so damned humiliating—after working all these years and fighting for my country . . . here I am standing in an unemployment line for hours all day. . . . I felt numb.

Interviewer: Was your wife supportive?

Otis: Oh yeah, about losing the job, I mean she knew I got screwed. I mean, a couple days after I lost my job some guys from the plant came to my house and said everyone supported me and would go to court for me. But I come to find out that they were told by the bosses to stay out of it. They were told in no uncertain terms that they would be terminated if they got involved. So that's the last I heard of anyone from my job.

Soon after Otis lost any hope of reaching twenty years on the job, he described suffering from serious depression. While he actually found another job with a collection agency and received some financial support from his wife's family, Otis soon returned to his old neighborhood and eventually into the throes of crack addiction.

Interviewer: So tell me what led you back the old neighborhood?

Otis: Because that's where I'm from. I never left. Only my time in the service and living with my wife, but I've always lived nearby. My closest friends are still there. People I grew up with who helped me out. I mean, both good times and bad times. And when things were bad we always drank together. . . . Typically, I'd go see my mom and pops every few weeks and then meet up with my buddies. My pops and I would have a few drinks and then crack started really hitting, so I started smoking and that was the beginning of the end for me.

Interviewer: Did your wife know you were using?

Otis: Yeah, she never seen me, but she knew. I mean we were married for many years. I mean we had problems with our marriage the whole time. She was a country girl from Virginia. And I'm a city boy. I drink and smoke; she never touched it. So we were totally, totally the opposite. It took a toll after awhile. . . . I remember the last night we were ever

> together was the night of that whole OJ Simpson Bronco chase. I was down in the basement watching the TV and using. And I woke her up, and we got into a shouting match and I hit her. And that was it. She told me, "If you ever hit me I'm gonna leave you." And that was it. She took our daughter and left.

Otis's wife never pressed charges against him. However, he would do several short bids behind bars for crack possession and his house was foreclosed. After a short stay with his parents, Otis learned through a friend who was a recovering substance abuser and fellow Vietnam veteran about the VA's Comprehensive Work Therapy (CWT) program. In order to qualify for CWT, a veteran suffering from drug and alcohol problem must agree to see a psychiatrist and is provided a tax-free, minimum wage job. Over the next year, Otis would work part-time at the VA washing pots and pans. However, growing increasingly restless with a job he described "as boring and pure hell," Otis eventually quit and went back on unemployment. Now destitute and suffering from numerous health problems, I asked Otis about his plans for the future:

Otis: Well, I finally put a claim in with the VA, but it's going through the bureaucracy. I'm looking to get some disability benefits, so I could live comfortably. I'm also on food stamps and I do get a small retirement check from my old job (the one where they fired me right before I hit twenty years). . . . But this is the first time I've ever truly been homeless. Trust me, the only time.

CHARLES: "YOU NEED TO EAT"

Charles returned from the service and moved back in with his foster parents. In the years after his return, he worked numerous jobs as a handyman, at a local hospital, as a U.S. Postal Service worker, and as an autoworker at the local Chrysler plant. However, abrupt changes in the economy created profound employment instability for Charles. He describes the economic downturn and the explosion of the street level drug economy in his neighborhood occurring almost simultaneously:

> Yeah I watched it change. Jobs dried up. But that was just the way it was. Factories shutting down even before I went in the service, so that was going on. But as far as quality of life, there was a period of time back in the '70s when you could leave your door open, like it is now. And go upstairs and go to bed. Nobody come in your house and take no TV set or nothing like that. They

> wasn't doing that kind of stuff. When the thing hit. . . . When the drug thing hit here, man everything starting going, you know bizarre. Drugs destroyed the neighborhood. That's why these houses are all boarded up now; they used to be full of dealers.

Interviewer: How did the drugs impact your life?

Charles: Say you doing bad, you not eating from month to month, around the middle of the month, you got no food in your house. But the crack dealer come around the house and say, "Here take this hundred dollars, go buy yourself some food." So you feel obligated to help him 'cause he help you get food, and he moves in just for a couple of days. And next thing you know they taken over the whole neighborhood.

In Charles's account it isn't that people chose to stop eating and then turn to funding crack dealers. It's that the profits of the neighborhood drug economy become the only form of survival in a community where work has vanished and has yet to return. Charles took me on a tour of the neighborhood, and I learned firsthand about this phenomenon in the neighborhood. The following exchange documents this excursion:

Interviewer: So those boarded-up buildings are where most of it was happening?

Charles: Yeah, this is where the dealers were.

Interviewer: Did you know any of the folks that lived there?

Charles: Sure. I knew everybody over here. Like I said you need to eat—you got to know who they are—and plus most of them were deep into using, too.

Interviewer: Where are they now?

Charles: Scattered around the city. Some dead, staying with family. Some did improve. You know some still doing it, you know what I mean? 'Cause it's crazy man, you figure I got out of the service forty-one years ago. I met guys that was messing with drugs when I got out of the service. Been on drugs for years. Here it is 2011, and I see them every day, they still on drugs. So I'm saying the only thing keeping them guys alive is drugs.

"PLEASE TAKE THE HOUSE"

Charles witnessed the ravages of poverty and the pains of addiction experienced by many in the neighborhood over a protracted period of time. Naturally, I was curious as to why he stayed in the community. As the following part of the interview illuminates, a collision of a family health crisis and economic calamity created an extraordinarily challenging situation that left Charles with few options.

Interviewer: Why did you stay here? When you were working did you ever, you know, when crack hit, and everything else, did you ever think about moving out of the community?

Charles: Out of this community, here? No, see my mom passed away. She had three strokes, and what I learned was Alzheimer's. I didn't recognize that's what she had. And after she passed away and everything started coming into focus, I realized she owed taxes for like four years and stuff like that, right. And water bills and stuff you know. And I didn't have the funds to handle it.

Interviewer: So they took the house?

Charles: No, I sold it to my nephew, because you know, I just couldn't handle it. Plus my roof had caved in and all my wall-to-wall carpet had buckled. It all buckled all through the house. Plus the walls are still messed up. And my nephew could do a lot of home improvements. So we talked and he was living in this apartment with five kids in a two bedroom apartment. And I said, "Why don't you take the house out off of me." He said, "I won't be able to pay this money off. I won't be able to pay off this money." He went over to talk to his wife and went to the bank and got a loan or something. I actually don't know what he did, but somehow he got the money. He came paid off all the taxes I owed on the house and paid the water bill off. So I said, "Please, take the house." I sold it to him real cheap.

In a desperate situation, when wealth becomes a liability, Charles was fortunate to have a family member who could take his deceased mother's home. This unexpected intergenerational transfer of debt presented Charles with an enormous challenge. Coupled with serious problems to his own home, he was left having to manage years of back taxes and bills on a property he inherited. Fortunately, his nephew was able to help him negotiate this difficult and potentially devastating situation. Charles had little savings of his own. As I learned, he was able to maintain a job for as long as a decade, but his own problems with addiction had caught up with him.

Interviewer: Why weren't you able to deal with the home problems through the VA? Or your retirement benefits?

Charles: I didn't go to the VA. I ain't ever used them except a little GI Bill, but I moved on, you know, after the military. Plus, I was working, but I couldn't hold a job down, because I messed up with drugs.

Interviewer: How did you get involved in drugs?

Charles: It was all over the place. And I was soft, soft to the game after I got home from the service. I didn't want to look like no lame guy. . . . I just thought it was a normal part of being home. You know, work and get high. But it didn't work out so good.

Interviewer: So it was the people you were around?

Charles: Yeah, I didn't realize I was getting older. And you know, put it this like this. A lot of white guys they come home, they gonna get married, buy homes. But black guys—living in a place like this where nothing comes easy—we weren't really thinking like that was in the cards for us. So, when we were around here it was just idle time wasting away getting high. But I tried to also work. . . . In the end, the drugs caught up with me.

"I FIND IT DISRESPECTFUL TO BE PROFILED"

The pains of poverty are taken for granted in the lives of black veterans such as Charles. For him, the so-called American Dream of marriage and homeownership simply didn't appear to be "in the cards." When I asked Charles whether or not he'd had any run-ins with the criminal justice system, his answer, as it does above, focuses on his experiences living in one of the most impoverished and aggressively policed locations in the city.

Interviewer: Did you have any runs-in with the law?

Charles: I was pretty lucky when I got home. Many people I knew got busted, but I kept a low profile, you know. But today—I'm really glad I'm clean and out of that life—because living here cops are always in your face. I get questioned all the time about drugs. I mean this a high drug area, so of course the cops are swarming around here to make their numbers. But I find it disrespectful to be profiled because I'm an older black man and Vietnam veteran. Cops be saying to me, "Come here." I say, "Yes sir, what's up?" And they like, "Don't Sir me! Where you going?" And I wasn't really going nowhere, this old man is just trying to take a walk down his street, you know? They say, "Why you walking down the street?" I say, "'Cause I live in this community. This is where I reside." And like they take my fingerprints and they don't have nothing on me. I mean, he says, "How the hell can you be from around here, and have no record?" It's stereotyping all the time around here like, "You black, you must have some time in jail." But I've never been in trouble in my life.

"I HAD TOO MUCH RESPONSIBILITY CARING FOR MY MOM"

Charles's story corresponds with an imposing literature that shows how "quality of life" or "zero tolerance" policing have altered life in the poorest, most racially segregated urban neighborhoods for the worse.[2] The simple act of talking a walk is fraught with heavy police surveillance. Moreover, the fact that Charles does not have a record is a source of surprise to the police rather than an opportunity for police to reach out to him as a someone to be respected in the community. Yet despite it all, Charles refuses to move. Indeed, he takes stubborn pride in the neighborhood as his community, a place that he and his family refuse to leave. Even though he battled with drugs and serious financial problems—although his wife continues to work and does provide some income for his family—Charles's post-military life is important for what it reveals about the limitations of military benefits in the lives of marginalized black veterans.

Interviewer: Did you use the GI Bill.?

Veteran: GI Bill, yeah. I did take some classes.

Interviewer: How'd that work out for you?

Veteran: I got some certificates from community colleges and stuff, but I didn't take advantage of it like I should have. Plus, I was working too and didn't have that college mindset. A lot of things I learned in life, I learned later in years. I regretted a lot I did, choices I made, you know.

As the next exchange reveals Charles's regrets are not simply the function of his addiction, but also a confluence of challenges, including, especially the responsibility of caring for a dying parent. While his mother's eventual death left him in a major financial calamity, interestingly, he attributes the experience of having to care for her as leading to his sobriety.

Interviewer: What did you regret? The drugs?

Charles: The drugs. The drugs was my thing. And then my foster mother got sick. The people that raised me, not my birth mother. She took sick. I had to take care of her. And that's how I got off drugs. I got out of that life for her. And since then—more than twenty-five years ago—I ain't never done drugs again.

Interviewer: Wow. . . . Tell me about that experience.

Charles: Well, first, I was not seeing the Alzheimer's and everything else that was wrong with her. I didn't know that, then one day she. . . . She did something that was real crazy. She called the fire department. She called the police department and the firemen came to the house. My neighbor across the highway called and said, "Charles you better get over here to your mom's house, 'cause something's going on there. You'd better get yourself over there." So, I put my sneakers on and run across the highway. I said, "Mom!" She says, "Charles! Charles! Come here! Where you been boy? I've been calling you? Where you at?" And my neighbors came over, one of them said, "Where the hell have you been?" And I said, "You better mind your own God damn business before I . . . you know, split your skull. I mean you got nothing to do with my mother's house. She my mom. This my mom's house." He said, "Well, you ain't doing shit for her. Get your mom some help! Get your mom some god damn help!" So, I went to the doctor the next day with her. . . . And then one day she went missing. . . . Then she was back in the psychiatric ward and started having strokes. And then things started closing in on me. I just felt like wanted to give up. . . . But I couldn't. She's my mom and I had to bathe her every day. That's why I eventually stopped getting high. You know what I'm saying now? I got no time for drugs. I had too much responsibility caring for my mom.

Interviewer: Do you remember the last time you used?

Charles: Oh yeah, I came home to my wife, I said, "[wife's name] I need you!" She says, "What?" I say, "Come here and walk, walk, walk, walk, walk with me." It was a joint that I didn't know was laced with rock (that's what they called crack back then). The first and last time I used it or any other drug. Man, I didn't know what was going on. I got scared and started panicking. The guy who gave me the joint told me it was laced, so I jumped out of the car and ran down the street. So when I got home to my wife—she's the love of my life to this day—she just walked with me around the whole neighborhood until I starting calming. Finally I came down.

"SHE STOOD BY ME WHEN I WAS AT MY LOWEST"

Charles's wife of forty-three years—in contrast to the majority of the black veterans I interviewed whose lives are characterized by marital instability—has been an enormously important form of support in his life. Here, Charles describes how they met and why he believes they've managed to stay together. Interestingly, it was his sister that introduced them.

Interviewer: Where did you meet your wife?

Charles: She was a young lady that hung around my sister. . . . And like my sister, she's active in the community. And she was kinda babysitting her kids while she was always at some meeting or some kind of event. And I used to come home to see my sister, I would see her, and we talked and the rest, as they say, was history [laughs]. Yeah she's a good one. She stood by me when I was at my lowest. She's a real good woman. . . . She still works in child care: just loves kids.

Charles also described his wife as playing an integral role in helping him care for his mother. Additionally, they take pride in their kids, even though growing up in the current environment is a challenge. Similar to Mel, Charles hopes one day that his children are able to travel and see the world beyond the neighborhood. As he describes:

> I hope my sons get to see more of the world. For me, that's what the military did most. I loved the experience of getting away from home. . . . And even after the service I worked as a guard down at the American Life Insurance Building. . . . And it's international; they have people from Japan, people from Germany coming in all the time. They came all to the building, and they took their lodging in the city. And when I was in the service in Okinawa after

> Vietnam, I picked up a little Japanese, so I could understand them a bit. I spoke to them, and got them around the hotel and around the city. . . . One night they gave me five hundred dollars! Back in them days that good money [laughs]! And I actually got a commendation for doing that you know. It was alright, man.

Much like Morris's experience (see chapter 2), Charles has a passion for travel. Learning some Japanese in Okinawa is not simply a story of transmitting social capital acquired in the military to the civilian workplace. Charles's exposure to other cultures in the military provides him with a wisdom that enables him to see a world beyond the streets, even many decades after serving in Okinawa. Additionally, his desire to have his sons see the world is driven by the desire to transmit social capital, without saying Charles dreams about a world for his children that is beyond the confines of the street and at once will provide them an experience that will have a lasting positive impact on the rest of their lives.

AVF ERA VETERANS ON THE HOME FRONT

Gerald

"I Slept with Styrofoam Egg Cartons on My Bedroom Floor"

Even though Gerald served in a dangerous combat role in Honduras, this experience was classified and he thus receives only a very small disability check from the VA. One benefit that he doesn't receive that has created havoc in Gerald's life is dental care. Throughout our interview Gerald clearly was in pain and clearly needed to see a dentist. As he stated, "Imagine this, here I am risking my life for my country and I can't even see a dentist! Man, it's crazy. There's a lot of pain, but I can't make any progress with them on this. No dental. The VA don't cover it for me." Gerald also suffered tremendously from PTSD in his first year back:

Gerald: Before I got help from the VA, I slept with Styrofoam egg cartons on my bedroom floor. And there were a couple times where I just crashed out on the living room floor and my mom stood back and hollered, "Wake up! Are you alright? Wake up!" One time she poked me with a broom handle you know because I'm hollering and screaming. Another time my brother-in-law thought it would be funny to play a trick on me. I fell asleep on the couch, and he thought it would be funny to come up and grab me and say, "Rooaaaarrr!" When I became conscious he was on

> the floor with my knee on his neck and I was getting ready to snap his neck. You know, I was like, "Don't ever, ever wake me up like that, don't ever do that. Don't ever sneak up on me, because I have a problem."

"That Was One of the Worst Days of My Life"

Recall in the previous chapter that Gerald described clear signs of deterioration in his neighborhood after returning home on leave. By the time he was discharged and moved back home, things had become exponentially worse. For one, many of his friends were now fully involved in street life, including his best friend who was struggling with substance abuse problems and had already done several bids in prison for drug-related charges. Gerald was witnessing the literal dissolution of his community around him, including the horrible murder of his sister.

Interviewer: Do you feel comfortable telling me about what happened to your sister?

Gerald: Three months before my father died, she came back on the scene and she went and stayed with my uncle in Atlantic City and she hooked up with a guy there. It's not completely clear, but we think she saw him commit a murder . . . because he shot her up with heroin and cocaine while she was asleep, gave her a hot shot and killed her. . . . She was only 35 years old. . . . She had three children. Yeah, that was pretty tough, that was one of the worst days of my life. We were really tight coming up, you know? And now I'm back from the service and she's dead.

In addition to his sister's tragic death, Gerald's older brother was also deep into street life. By the time Gerald returned home from the service he had done several bids in prison. Indeed, at the time of our interview, Gerald's brother was currently serving time. Yet for many years Gerald was able to keep himself insulated from the perils of street life that had consumed so many around him.

Interviewer: How were you able to keep yourself out of that life?

Gerald: My mom got me a job. So I was able to work for two years without incident.

Interviewer: What happened?

Gerald: I just got fed up with the place and I couldn't stay there. It was a corporate job and I just couldn't do it anymore, you know take orders from this cat that I'm smarter than.

"I Just Can't Have People Afraid of Me Anymore"

After quitting his job, Gerald finally caved into the temptations of the underground economy. He went from the "courier thug" he described himself becoming in the deadly jungles of Honduras to now being tempted by the lure of the streets. Indeed, Gerald describes his experience in the military as "preparation" for his this next phase in his life—what he described as a "con man." In contrast to his friends and neighbors, whom he described as being swallowed up by the drug war, Gerald took on a much more covert role in street life:

Gerald: I wasn't getting involved directly in the drug game. I did street-level financing like loan sharking, which was pretty lucrative.

Interviewer: How did the military prepare you for being a loan shark?

Gerald: I didn't have a conscience and I had seen it all. But I also knew dead men don't pay bills, so I wouldn't kill you, but I'd break your arm depending on how much you'd owe. . . . I could remember people asking me what happens if I don't have your money. We'll break that arm when we come to it, was usually my stock answer. . . . Most of the time I lean into gamblers, because I learned gamblers will pay. They pay the interest but they don't pay the principle, which works great for me because they paid the interest to me every week. So it was real lucrative. The gamblers they got to get on the table, you know? So they'll take another loan, which doubles their interest. So that's just the nature of the beast.

Gerald's stint as a loan shark was short-lived. After both his parents found out and, as he describes it, "considered me dead to the family," he knew he had to get out.

Interviewer: How were you able to make the break?

Gerald: I shut down the loan sharking and turned it over to a couple of my boys. But I also really didn't like the person I had become. I mean, some pretty hard people were scared of me. And one day, I said it to one of my boys, "I can't believe that all these cats are that scared of me." And they said, "Shit man, we're scared of you. Everybody's scared of you." So, I'm like, "Are you kidding?" And they're like, "No, you pumping fear in a lot of people," and I said okay this had got

	to stop, you know. I just can't have people afraid of me anymore. And my paranoia only worsened. So that's when I first went to the VA and talked to a counselor about PTSD.
Interviewer:	So what happened next?
Gerald:	Well, somebody suggested that I join the American Legion because I would find other vets to talk to, and that's what I did. I joined the American Legion, I actually became the second vice commander of the American Legion for two years and what have you. . . . And that helped me a lot because a lot of the older cats would talk to me and what have you and they showed a lot of faith in me. No one had showed that much faith in me since I had been a teenager. So that helped a lot and it helped a lot with the paranoia and it definitely helped with the withdrawal you know and with the bouts of withdrawal.

Gerald's involvement with the American Legion was a life changing experience for him. Not only did he regain a sense of self-respect that was long missing from his life, he began to take his recovery more seriously. Like other African-American veterans, Gerald also became deeply involved in his church. However, similar to Vietnam era veteran Charles's situation, Gerald's own recovery quickly gave way to mounting family responsibilities, including caring for his mother who eventually succumbed to complications from breast cancer.

Interviewer:	Did you ever consider moving away after your mom died?
Gerald.	Well, no. I mean had to put all of my energies into caring for my mother. I stayed with her for a long time. If anything I grew more attached to this place. I mean, this is my home you know and I like it here.

"It Was Real and It Was My Journey"

In a remarkable turn of events, after all the tragedies Gerald endured, it was not until relatively recently that he would find a new calling. Nearing the end of our interview, I asked him about what he envisions doing in the future. It was in this exchange that I learned about Gerald's passion for writing, including work he had done as a journalist for a black newspaper and several book projects he is currently involved in.

Gerald:	You know, um, it's been a rough journey, but it was real and it was my journey. I wouldn't be who I am now if I hadn't went through what I went through, you know? Plus, beginning in the

> late '90s I got a job in the printing business and met my mentor. He was a very pivotal person in my life because he got me to write. I don't think I would be a writer if I didn't go through all of this. Writing is really something that's very important to me, you know. It's really a part of who I am, you know, and I don't know who I'd be without that, you know, because it has brought so much to my life. I've spoken in front of city council, I've done some acting, music production, and all that came from writing, you know?

Although Gerald is unemployed, he continues to constantly write and is a self-professed "political junky." Indeed, he describes it as a crucial part of his ongoing struggle with PTSD:

> Right now it's pretty tough being out of work. I'm living with my cousin for financial reasons more than anything. And there are just times when the paranoia comes, you know? But I can't sleep more than about four hours at a stretch, anyway. So I'm up writing. And I'll turn on political programs, I'm a political junkie, so that helps a lot too. It helps me to direct my anger. I mean it's been a while since I woke up screaming or, you know, sweating or whatever. It's been a while since that's happened and that's a good thing. . . . So, I make it work, you know, I deal with it. And it works, I watch Morning Joe in the morning even though it's a bunch of Republicans that piss me off [laughter].

Despite the many post-military challenges in Gerald's life, he is able to come to terms with his own destiny after a turn to street life as a loan shark confronts him with a disturbingly callous side of himself that he can no longer accept. He first turns to the church for support, but like Charles is quickly thrown into the role of caretaker for his dying mother. Gerald simply no longer has time to be a "street tough." Most poignant is how his discovery of writing provides him with a diverse array of social capital that enables him to have relief from PTSD, enables him to increase ties with his community (e.g., speaking to city council), and draws him closer to the political world around him. Beyond a trivial escape, Gerald's engagement with politics through various media reveals a stronger sense of self-efficacy. No longer a "courier thug," he describes a more direct engagement with the bigger world around him.

Gregory

"I Was Stuck"

After Gregory returned to Delaware, he continued detailing cars. He enjoyed some success, even securing several contracts with local auto dealerships in the area. However, after five years, Gregory once again yearned for different surroundings. Like Charles, his time in the military gave him a direct experience with a world much bigger than Wilmington. After recently returning to Delaware to help with the care of a sick parent, Gregory was contacted by a long estranged ex-girlfriend in Florida about a child he had lost touch with many years ago. According to Gregory, his ex-girlfriend wanted him to drive to Florida and meet his daughter; apparently it had been nearly a decade since he had seen her. Unbeknownst to him, however, his ex-girlfriend's invitation to reconnect with family in Florida had an important ulterior motive—namely, she sought back child support that Gregory had never intended on paying. But a warrant had been issued for his arrest nearly nine years ago—indeed, soon after his estranged daughter had been born. He describes his subsequent arrest, and the impounding of his vehicle after a night spent sleeping in his car in a Florida rest stop:

> I'm driving down there and I pulled into a rest stop to get some sleep and fell asleep in my car, and when I woke it was morning. The police were right behind me and she says, "What's going on?" And I said, "Nothing, I'm just driving home and I was tired so I pulled over to get some sleep instead of causing an accident . . . . So she said, "Let me see your ID." So I gave her my ID, I didn't think anything of it. She came back and said "You know there is a warrant for your arrest?" I said, "Stop playing." She said, "Yup, you got to come with me." So they impounded my car with all my stuff in it. I mean they took my dog and locked me up for three weeks. By the time I got out, I lost my dog, lost my car, lost all my belongings. And I was stuck.

After he was released on bond, Gregory stayed in a homeless shelter in Florida. Shortly thereafter his sister offered to pay his bus fare back and he subsequently returned to Delaware. His sister even let him stay at her house for a few weeks. Gregory described his new living arrangement as problematic. Apparently, his sister and her boyfriend struggled with addiction. However, a serious foot injury limited his housing options.

Interviewer: So what happened when you got back to your sister's house?

Gregory: It was real sketchy. I mean I knew she had a lot of problems with dope, but I didn't have any alternatives, so I remember coming into her place. And it's all torn up with nails and old rotted boards everywhere, trash everywhere, and that first night I stepped on a nail and it messed my foot up.

Interviewer: So did you go to the doctor?

Gregory: No, I don't have any insurance. So I'm pretty much trapped there and then I wasn't getting the proper care at her house because I couldn't let my foot breathe. And I couldn't eat right. They barely eat all day and then was cooking dinner late at night. I'm like that ain't the way you supposed to eat. You supposed to eat three consecutive times a day: breakfast, lunch and dinner. And they would eat whenever and whatever; both my sister and her boyfriend were also using drugs so they ate when they came off the high or whatever. And that wasn't me, I didn't use.

After Gregory's foot becomes infected his next plan is to go to the emergency room. However, in a sudden turn of events, his sister's boyfriend is arrested. Shaken by the news, Gregory describes his sister as very depressed "almost suicidal." So, he decides to forego going to the emergency room in order to stay with her. Finally, in excruciating pain, Gregory's sister takes him to the hospital. While he is there, his sister posts bond for her boyfriend and begins to try and find a shelter for Gregory to stay in when he returns from the hospital.

Gregory: And I said, look I am not living like that. So, I'm laying there in the hospital and she called me up and said where you going when you get out of the hospital? I said, "I thought I was coming back there to stay with you." And she's like, "Oh no, you can't come back here." I said. "What?" She said, "No you can't come back here. Because your foot needs to heal and that smell, I ain't putting up with that." So I said, "Alright, no problem." That's what I told her in the hospital, I said look, got nowhere to go. So that's how I became homeless. Because when I was staying with my sister she told me I can't come back there, so that's homeless.

"I Wanna Make Money"

After a few days in emergency care, Gregory was transferred to the VA hospital and eventually to IH. Since his time at IH, he has spent most days alone. No longer speaking to his sister, Gregory's only family in the area were his parents, who had apparently both recently passed away. He aspires to return to Florida, but is very wary of returning until he is no longer homeless:

> But when I got arrested down there, everything changed. They hate the homeless in Florida. I mean everybody that I talked to who was homeless down there was like, "Man, when I came here, I didn't have a record. Now that I have been here its a rap sheet a mile long." It's like anywhere in public you go the cops target you. I can't go back there. I ain't taking the chance of messing my life up, 'cuz I don't have a record. So, once I can come get myself together up here—get me a job, make me some money—then I'll consider going back to Florida.

In response to my question regarding his plans for the future, Gregory explains:

> Well you know what, I am going to get back to Florida to succeed. Because everything up here is hard. Negotiating is hard; people are hard. So, I've been on the Internet, I have been calling people and talking to people down in Florida already. . . . I got a company I'm working with down there, and I am what you consider a locator. I locate the properties, I inspect the properties, I get a contractor to look at the property then I turn the property to them. . . . My plan, is to go back in a week. . . . I got my bus ticket already. And all my friends are like, "Why are you going back to Florida?" And I'm like, "I wanna make money." You know, I can sit up here in the projects, and do like everybody else. I can feel sorry for myself. I can live on Section 8 and get a little government check. But I can't see myself doing that. I like too many things. I like nice clothes. I like eating right.

Gregory's post-military story is one of a veteran who continues to be caught between two worlds. On the one hand, he has experienced, at least temporarily, upward mobility in the military and after his return to Delaware. But his irresponsibility as a deadbeat dad catches up with him and creates a sudden and powerful downward spiral into poverty and homelessness. Now back in Delaware he is dependent on a sister who provides him temporary shelter but is clearly not a reliable member of his kin network. Yet Gregory's debilitating foot injury and lack of employment leaves him with few options except an eventual move into temporary housing at IH. His desire to acquire financial capital and leave Delaware is quite analogous to his original departure for the military. Gregory longs for the lifestyle he once had, and his past experience with upward mobility serves as the catalyst for his future ambitions as financially independent and no longer in a place he associates with a kind of social inertia that comes with reliance on public assistance; clearly he has internalized stereotypes associated with a "lazy" black welfare poor. Despite his own destitution, Gregory adapts to his situation with a ruthless desire to move onward and hopefully upward.

FROM DISCHARGE TO PRISON

The role of prison in the lives of AVF era African-American veterans is particularly pervasive. In this era of mass imprisonment, young African-American men are locked up in astonishing numbers. It is thus not surprising that several of the respondents described incarceration as a pervasive part of their post-military experience. In this section, I detail the experiences of several veterans previously introduced and also include others who provided unique insight into their post-military-to-prison experiences. In what follows, veterans' prison stories are precipitated by especially difficult experiences with the VA, disputes with landlords, assaults of girlfriends and loved ones, and failure to pay child support that lead them into entanglements with the criminal justice system. Yet as in the other veterans' stories, prolonged unemployment and a lack of strong social networks and social capital are invariably a prominent backdrop against which pathways into incarceration are formed. In short, veterans' stories of incarceration are complex and not easily explained by any one variable or set of conditions.

"WE CAN'T GET A JOB, SO WE JUST SURVIVING OUT HERE"

After nine long months in Iraq, Andre's career in the military came to an abrupt and devastating end. After receiving a Bad Conduct Discharge (BCD), Andre struggled to find work.

After two years of countless rejections from employers, Andre had run out of options. Additionally, he had lost contact even with the marines he had developed such a strong bond with over the years, including a former sergeant who hired him to work temporarily as a roofer:

> I've lost contact with my brothers, most of 'em you know. I mean I had one brother in the Marine Corps who was my boss at work—he got me a couple of jobs roofing after Iraq—he stood by me even after they threw me out. But that didn't last. I haven't heard much from him since.

Andre describes another Iraq veteran he met on the streets, who was in a similar situation. For him, the experience of being with other homeless black veterans has made him especially critical of white society:

> He's in the same situation: we can't get no job, so we out here surviving. But I'm starting to think there's nothing out here for us. In this white society, I either got to carry a microphone, a bottle, or a gun. Soldier, a rapper, or entertainer. Or playing some kind of sport or a boxer or a fighter or something. But it's not gonna happen. I mean so many of us don't have jobs or are in the

street. . . . And don't even get me started on that's credit card bills and we ain't even talking about eating. I know what it's like to be a veteran and have nothing to eat, you know what I'm saying?

Andre believes that consumer culture has been especially toxic to African-Americans in the United States.

But what people take for granted be stuff like cable and stuff like that. For black people, that's creating more problems for ourselves. You see what I'm saying? You already don't have the money to hardly live in the first place. But now we just wanna live like everybody else and be so-called happy. But we don't even know what that is without spending money.

When asked about whether or not there's anyone who has helped with the financial challenges in his life, Andre explains:

So, for me to lean on them would actually put more on them, you know what I'm saying? I already know they living check to check. I means it's just like every black person I know. So I can't get myself to ask for money. No.

Like many other veterans I interviewed, Andre describes his mother as the single most supportive person in his life (e.g., "she's my rock"):

When I got a tat she's like, "What is this mess, you and all these tattoos," and then she read her name, she was like, "Oh, I kind of like this." I said, "You better" [laughs]. Any money I can make I spend it on my momma. African necklaces, you know what I'm saying? The kind of jewelry that was made for an African queen. But mom has always had a job and has supported me financially. I always wanted to build her a house. . . . And it ain't even about being rich; it's about just being able to live. And if I didn't get thrown out of the Marine Corps, I would be able to just live.

Andre's first brush with the law came after being arrested on a driving under the influence (DUI) charge. Apparently, he was taking a few college courses and missed his court date:

Yeah, they came with a warrant and pulled me out of class. And I was in jail for seven days. . . . Just long enough to get kicked out. So even when I've tried to get back on track, there's always something.

Now living on the streets, Andre began to sell marijuana to eat. Soon thereafter he was arrested in a sting and did a year in prison:

I was able to keep a low profile so the time pretty much just flew by. I mean it was hard to go through, but I knew they couldn't hold me forever. But life is different for black people when they go to jail. Because they hold you on all

> these fines. And a white person's got money, so the white people I see in the joint aren't scared, they're not tripping. They thinking, "Oh I got a couple of fines to take care of. First I'll take care of bail and then I'll just pay the magistrate and then I'll just pay whatever little fines that they got going on and now I can't party for a couple of weekends." I've seen it with my own eyes. It's all about money and paying fines. But me and my brothers, we're broke. So for us, it's serious. I'm not gonna get to see nobody and nobody's gonna be able to come get me out. That's the worst feeling: I don't have the money to get out of jail, I don't have the money to pay these fines.

Andre believes the numerous fines imposed on prisoners is especially unjust in the case of veterans:

> For a veteran to go through something like this!? It shouldn't happen. We're barely surviving, especially if you're cut off from benefits like I am. I mean, it's a sick system they've got.

In another instance, Andre is arrested for illegal possession of a firearm. Apparently, he had started his own side business repairing jewelry. One day he was wearing one of the gold chains he repaired and a homeless person he just gave a dollar to "snatched it off my neck":

> So after that I bought me a gun, a small little .22, one of them "get up off me" guns. I took it with me to my girlfriend's house, and I didn't plan on driving her car that day. My license was already suspended, but she asked me to drive her car. So at that point I had a decision to make, you know. I could leave the gun at her house where she's got kids and one of them could possibly get it. So I took the gun with me. So, I'm going to go get her from work, and I run out of gas. I pulled the vehicle over, I open a couple of doors cause it's hot, I try to call her to get the wrecker to come out and give me some gas. She can't make that happen. I called her mother. She can't make anything happen. And then my phone died. I'm sitting here stuck at this point—no gas, no power to the phone, the thing won't work or nothing. I do have the charger though, but the thing won't work. I see the cop coming toward me, I'm already like well no sudden moves. I see how he's looking at me. So, I sit on the passenger seat, mind you the doors are still open right and I say, "Sir, do you mind helping me out, I just need to get some gas so I can get to where I'm going. I got to pick my girl up from work. He told me to have a seat, and he called out the K9 unit. The next thing I know there's more cops and before I know it I'm in handcuffs going back to jail.

"WE'LL JUST TAKE THINGS DAY BY DAY"

Andre's post-military experience has become precisely what Gregory fears: a growing criminal record and precipitous fall into poverty. In contrast to Gregory's lust for the capitalist dream, Andre has become thoroughly disenchanted by the money chase. On the one hand, Andre voices a broad critique of a runaway consumerism that he sees as particularly harmful to the black community. Yet Andre's experiences with the prison's aggressive system of fines reveals that the financial burdens he describes as negatively impacting the broader African-American community is a deeply personal experience for Andre. At the same time, he maintains a strong relationship with his mother and contemplates his future:

> I'm thinking about a cosmetology degree—because I enjoy cutting hair—I did everyone's hair in the military. But I also love hip hop music, rapping, and writing lyrics. So I want to keep my options open, but I'm thinking I got a future in entertainment. But we'll just take things day by day.

"I WAS BROKE DOWN TO NOTHING IN THERE"

After ending his military career locked down in the harsh conditions of a Marine Corps brig, Terrence returned to civilian life. After only a year, he got a job driving a truck but shortly thereafter he got a DUI. At the time, Terrence was living with his brother and girlfriend in a decrepit housing project in one of the city's most impoverished and intensely policed sections. It was at this time that Terrence had his first encounter with crack cocaine:

> I noticed that my brother and his girlfriend was always in this back room, always quiet. And I got curious and I went back there. I was a smoker. I smoked cigarettes. I saw them back there smoking this stuff. That's when I got introduced to it. And I got hooked. So for the past ten years, I've been in and out rehabs, halfway houses, and prison.

I asked Terrene to describe to me the first time he was incarcerated:

> I just got banned from the VA. I was suffering from depression and PTSD and got up in one of the counselor's faces. So they cut me off. I had no medication. Nothing. So I got a bunch of crack and passed out in my car. The next thing you know I'm in the back of a police car. And I wound up doing almost two years. It was crazy in there. I mean it's all young black men. Guys younger than me. And I got stabbed and thrown in the hole. I lost like twenty pounds in there. Sleeping in my own shit and piss. I was broke down to nothing in there.

Interviewer: How did you survive?

Terrence: It's interesting because that's where I first really got in touch with religion. We had a serious bible study. And I just put all my faith in the Lord. So I survived because of God. And that's how I'm surviving to this very day.

Like many other respondents, religion is an essential form of "survival capital" in Terrence's life. Finding God gives him the will to survive. Interestingly, Terrence's life in recent months has taken a positive turn. While at IH he began to put his plumbing skills to work doing various jobs for private homeowners who pay him under the table. More recently, Terrence has reconnected with his birth father, who owns his own plumbing business. Additionally, Terrence has been aggressive in his recovery. In addition to attending therapy at the VA, he also was recently awarded state disability benefits, which provides a much needed financial boost. While he has no plans to leave IH, Terrence does seem to be on a positive track in all aspects of his life.

"I GOT NAILED BY AN UNDERCOVER COP"

Another AVF era veteran, Arthur (age 43), who lived only blocks away from Terrence, described a similar set of conditions precipitating his incarceration. However, like Jackson, the death of his mother began his downward spiral, which began with destitution, homelessness, crack addiction, and finally prison.

Interviewer: So when did your mom die?

Arthur: I was living at home. And I went and knocked on the bedroom door, and there wasn't any answer, you know. So I go downstairs and I'm watching TV. And my father, the first thing he likes to do in the morning is go walking. He goes somewhere, and he walks. And he came back, and I'm downstairs, and I hear him say, "Come here! Come here! Come here!" I go upstairs. My mom was laid out, she was in the bed, she was dead.

Interviewer: My gosh. . . . Do you mind telling me what happened afterward?

Arthur: Some people came to check her out. Doctors and stuff. And I helped them sit her up. And they was with their stethoscopes going [inaudible]. And my father, he was downstairs, and he was in the back. I heard him crying. Then they left and more people come and took her body away. . . . And say about four or five months later my father met another lady and he married her. And then she died [laughs].

Interviewer: No.

Arthur: Yes, and that's when my dad changed. He was like, "Leave, leave, leave." And I'd be downstairs watching TV and I know he's in the house. So one day, he said, "I'll be back, I'll be back, I'll be back." And I wouldn't see him 'til the next day. And then he told me he sold the house. He got rid of the house. I was the last one there. He said, "Go through all your drawers and get your stuff ready." And I said, "Yeah, okay." So, I came home when he was there, I went and got everything out of the room, and we got out. Then he brought me across the bridge to the Salvation Army. And he says, "Well, I'm gonna leave you here." And then he went on with his merry way.

Interviewer: So what happened at the Salvation Army?

Arthur: It was a nightmare there. I hated it. And I also lost my job at the time, so I was in the streets most of the time and I got locked up.

Interviewer: What happened?

Arthur: Possession of drugs. Cocaine. I got nailed by an undercover cop. I mean, especially in the late 80s this area was nothing but drugs. And I went up there one time and said, "What's up, man?" And he said, "Yo, how much you want?" I took two rocks. And as soon as I got back to my house, I got busted right there. And I did eight months.

Interviewer: What was the prison like?

Arthur: Where I was, 'cause I really don't talk to people that much, I was in a cell with two people that was already in there. I thought I would be in a cell by myself. One guy had six years and one guy had four to five years. And as soon as I put my—called my name and told me what cell I was in. I said, man hasn't even seen me and told me where I'm gonna be. And I went in a cell, and I slept on the floor for eight months. It was the worst experience of my life and my back is still screwed up from sleeping on that concrete floor.

In contrast to Charles, when Arthur lost his mother his life began to deteriorate. Indeed, this tragedy leads to the veritable dissolution of his family. For reasons never fully disclosed, Arthur's father now sees him as simply expendable. Like Martin's father who dumps all his belongings on the curb (see chapter 2), Arthur is also determined to be no longer of any use. Rather than organize any meaningful opportunities for grieving and support, Arthur's father drops him off at the Salvation Army. Now destitute after losing his job, Arthur plunges deeper into despair. Feeling profoundly alienated and alone, he turns to the streets. Like so many young black men of his generation, poverty and street life quickly lead to entanglements with criminal justice system. Yet after his parole, Arthur got a job doing landscaping and recently moved out of IH. Indeed, my interview took place the day before he was to move out:

> It was good timing too, because I was starting to get fed up here. I had been relying on my military routines—getting up early and trying to do some push-ups—you know keep things structured. But people only care about themselves. They keep their TVs on loud at night so it's hard to get a good night's sleep. And just about everybody smokes—I quit a month or so ago—but it's hard around here to get anything positive going. But I'm lucky to have a job now and this new apartment is outside the city, so it's all good, you know what I'm saying?

Chapter Six

"We Thank You for Your Service"

> I mean, it had all been a few weeks after I arrived at IH. And here I am walking down the street in this seedy section of Wilmington blowing off some steam. I knew I had blew it by drinking a few beers. But all of the sudden these cops just start coming out of nowhere in all directions, arresting everyone on the block. I got taken away in the paddy wagon for public drunkenness but bailed myself out the next day, and then checked myself into Coatesville [Pennsylvania VA Hospital]. I mean, it's two years later [2009] and I'm sober but there's still a bench warrant out for my arrest.
>
> —Carl (age 64), Vietnam era veteran

Carl somehow believed that checking himself into Coatesville might clear him of the public drunkenness charges. But more than two years later, he was pulled over for a traffic violation in a leased vehicle with temporary license plates and was notified by police that he was still wanted by the authorities in Wilmington. According to Carl, police issued a ticket but did not arrest him because "they saw my Vietnam veterans hat with the Purple Heart insignia. . . . I think they let me go because I was a veteran. And now I got the summons to appear in court."

I learned all of this in a telephone conversation with Carl the previous day. Now I was at IH with a typed letter of support in hand. I agreed to accompany Carl to his hearing. We sat down in IH's computer room, and he pulled out a soft leather briefcase stuffed with papers. As Carl informed me: "Look at all of these letters and VA records. I want to put my best foot forward in front of the judge." Just prior to leaving for the Wilmington courthouse, I had a chance to peruse these materials and managed to transcribe some of the language in my field notes:

A VA counselor: "Carl has been exemplary in his treatment. In the many years I've known him he has never missed an appointment. . . . I've worked with many combat veterans with PTSD and Carl is one of the most committed to his recovery."

The director of a temporary housing program: "Carl is well respected by everyone who lives here. Not only does he follow the guidelines of the program, but he serves as a mentor to younger veterans. . . . On numerous occasions, Carl has literally walked several men through each step of their VA paperwork. We are lucky to have Carl in this program."

A copy of an opinion by the U.S. Court of Veterans Appeals: "It is obvious that this veteran has struggled with addiction. . . . This court has noted on several occasions that substance abuse is not grounds for the disqualification of disability benefits—indeed, it is extremely common among combat veterans of the Vietnam era. . . . In addition to his lengthy history of addiction, this veteran suffers from PTSD as the result of combat duty in Vietnam and also is infected with the HIV virus. . . . Given these serious health problems, we see no justifiable reason that he should lose disability benefits and therefore deny the recommendation before us."

I was especially curious about the court opinion.

Carl: "Yeah, that court opinion was a doozy . . . ! I had just gotten out of prison on a drug charge and the VA decided that they were gonna randomly reduce my disability benefits. So, I got a lawyer and kicked their butts [laughs]!

By this time, we had talked for nearly two hours: Carl and I had to scramble to my car to make it to his hearing on time. "Time to face the music," Carl said as we sat in a downtown Wilmington courtroom awaiting the judge's ruling.

To describe what happened at the hearing as surreal would be an understatement. When we first arrived, I realized we were in a drug and alcohol diversion court. The dozen or so offenders waiting to have their cases heard were at least half Carl's age (e.g., young men and women in their late 20s and early 30s). Their cases were quickly dispensed with by the judge, as one-by-one they were ordered into treatment. The public defender took one look at Carl's case, and after a brief meeting with the judge informed us, "Okay, he would like to address your case at the very end, after everyone has left the room." Fortunately, it only took little more than an hour until the courtroom had emptied. The judge asked Carl to approach the bench and then said, "Let me take a another look at the paperwork you have provided." Next, he asked Carl if he would like to make a statement. Without hesitation, Carl approached the microphone directly facing the judge and stated:

> Your Honor, I greatly appreciate the willingness of this court for providing me the opportunity to speak. As you can see from my records, I have been through a lot in my life, especially since returning from service in Vietnam. I've made many mistakes and I won't deny that. But Your Honor, as you can see from the letters and [turning to me] the professor's letter and his presence in this courtroom with me today, that I am making a lot of progress in my recovery. I am 100 percent committed to my recovery. I thank Your Honor for the opportunity to address this court.

I was stunned by Carl's composure. He spoke calmly and also with authority. At this point, I was convinced that everything would be okay, but my heart still raced as I awaited the judge's response. After a few more glances at Carl's paperwork, the judge asked, "Sir, you are responding to a warrant that was issued more than two years ago, correct?" Carl nodded. "You do know, by the letter of the law, I should remand you right at this moment. . . . I could have you taken directly from this courtroom to prison, do you understand that sir?" Carl nodded. "While we thank you for your service and your positive efforts at recovery, this case is very peculiar. . . . But given your demonstrated commitment to recovery, I'm not going to remand you at this time. However, you will have to meet with the drug counseling team here to schedule your treatment program. And if you test positive—if your urine test comes up positive just once, sir—I will have you taken into custody immediately, do you understand?" Carl nodded and thanked the judge.

I was obviously relieved by the outcome. At the same time, the day was an emotional whirlwind, one I was simply not prepared for. I had no idea just how serious Carl's situation was. But after dropping Carl off, I had to race to campus to teach an afternoon class and, at least, for the rest of the day, forgot all about the hearing. Yet that evening I could not stop thinking about the judge's words, *"We thank you for your service."* Yes, the judge gave Carl a break "by the letter of the law." But to "thank" someone in an instant for life experiences so profoundly impacted by a brutal war and its terrible aftermath in a word, troubled, me. Like most veterans I too appreciate being thanked for my service by non-veterans. But thinking about those words in a broader sociological context left them devoid of meaning for me.

Veterans' complex needs are rarely debated in a way that takes broader social conditions, such as housing policies, into account. Indeed, it is our *collective forgetting* of veterans' painful if not, devastating, journeys home that simply cannot be captured by words of "support" or "thanks." No amount of flag waving or homecoming parades can gloss over generations of veterans who struggle to survive in America's most impoverished and racially aggrieved neighborhoods. Reflecting on the nearly four years I have spent with African-American veterans hidden away in some of the most disadvantaged places I have ever visited has only solidified my belief that honoring veterans' service symbolically—no matter how important such rituals may be—does little to actually *support* the enormous needs of veterans.[1] To the contrary, the nation *betrays* veterans precisely because of ignorance to the quiet brutality they endure on a daily basis.

BEYOND "THE RIGHT TO SURVIVE"

The purpose of a small book like this ultimately is to go deeper into the lives of veterans like Carl, a survivor of Jim Crow era racism, a decorated African-American Vietnam veteran, recovering HIV+ substance abuser, and simultaneously a loving grandfather. A man who has benefitted greatly from the VA as well as the bond he maintains with his incredibly supportive ex-wife, Pauline. Or Andre, a young veteran of the recent Iraq War who struggles to confront the burdens of the war at home. Despite his negative discharge, he is a survivor who loves his mother and hopefully will rebound from the many burdens in his young life. Or Earl, a Vietnam era veteran who struggles to free himself from the pains of addiction and a life on the streets. At the same time, he maintains a deep connection with his daughter, advises his grandson with love and candor, and he longs for the day when he can treat him to a soda and a bag of chips. Or Gerald, an AVF era veteran who survived the racist maelstrom of the busing backlash of the 70s, confronted his own post-military struggles with street life, and eventually found his calling as a writer. Or Charles, a Vietnam era veteran who, as a conscript returning to Camp Lejeune endured the racist oppression of a white mob, survived the perils of a combat theater while working in an especially dangerous ammunition dump, returned from the service to watch his neighborhood plunge into economic turmoil and desperation, overcame his own addiction, and along with his supportive wife, cared for his mother right up until her passing. Charles, moreover, remains proud to be a lifelong resident of a "high crime" neighborhood, even if living there means going for a casual stroll risks being confronted by aggressive law enforcement.

The life stories of these African-American veterans, and many others like them, form the bedrock of this book. Taken together, their stories are a compelling tale of struggle and resilience, even in the face of tremendous social deficits. While not all respondents feel entitled to readjustment and health benefits, the majority have at least found some assistance from the VA. But it is sobering to remember that such entitlements are still very much in their organizational infancy. When Vietnam era veterans returned home, there were no "veteran's rights." Indeed,there were none until 1978, when Senator Allen Cranston's legislation secured the first federal funding for the nation's vet centers. Yet as Gerald Nicosia compellingly argues in his comprehensive history, *Home to War: A History of the Vietnam Veteran's Move-*

ment, the 1980s were a "decade of betrayal" for veterans. The U.S. Senate larded entitlements with complex bureaucratic red tape that made accessing them increasingly difficult. Although in subsequent decades the VA has become "a kindler and gentler bureaucracy,"[2] the experience of impoverished African-American veterans confined to ghettoized communities has, by all accounts, not resulted in more equality or inclusion. The aspiration of "black veteran's rights" as a 1993 Congressional Committee hearing on "African-American Veterans and Community" illuminated is far from being realized.[3]

Veteran centers remain paranoid, reactive, overcrowded, and understaffed bureaucracies in the twenty-first century. [4] One of their biggest shortcomings is that they have no local organization or presence in the community. In this way, the VA is a bureaucracy that veterans must seek out on their own accord. However, as this book has shown, veterans of the Vietnam and AVF eras return to worsening conditions in nearly every aspect of their individual and collective lives. Veterans like Charles and Gerald describe with obvious personal difficultly—indeed, both were noticeably withdrawn or agitated when talking about the veritable disintegration of their communities (e.g., the physical deterioration of housing and the swallowing up of their neighbors and family members by the drug war). When talking about what they've witnessed, it is clear their experiences, as Erikson so succinctly explains, must be seen as part of "a gradual realization that the community no longer exists as *an effective source of support*."[5] Moreover, these stories of collective trauma are juxtaposed with visceral stories of individual trauma; many respondents, such as Vietnam era veteran Earl, describe a turn of events that leads nearly to their own self-destruction. Carl's story serves perhaps as the ultimate example: he describes a decline in his health as a perverse "blessing in disguise" (see chapter 4), as now he has "easier access" to VA health care. In effect, Carl and other chronically ill veterans must "get worse" to "get better."

In no post-military story presented in this book do we learn of the VA as playing a genuinely pro-active role in the ordinary lives of marginalized African-American veterans. To the contrary, the VA is a place of last resort or virtually non-existent in their lives. Taken together their stories are testimony to the broader systems of oppression that, in a word, *overwhelm* any genuine experience of rights or entitlements in respondents' lives. Indeed, when black veterans or their children are ensnared in the criminal justice system, are left to live in horribly substandard housing conditions, or are forced to confront addiction alone, it is clear that "entitlement to benefits" is a phrase less about evoking one's rights than it is a declaration of survival.

When considering the problem of veteran's rights further, an important shortcoming of this book is illuminated; my study focuses only on African-American *male* veterans. Given the increasing numbers of veterans who are women of color, gender must be a central part of any serious strategies for addressing the inequalities presented throughout this book. Indeed, the intersections of race, class, and gender are presented here—with the exception of my interview with Carl's ex-wife Pauline—illuminated from a black male-centered perspective only. African-American male veterans admit to abusing their wives and neglecting to pay critical child support payments. But I've only presented one side of the story which, distressingly, is described by male respondents as almost an afterthought: "I smacked her around;" "I hit her, and then she left me." Given that studies document higher incidents of battering among veterans,[6] it is clear that the missing voices of female survivors is a serious omission in this book. I can only hope that future research attends to the experiences of black female veterans and the girlfriends, partners, and spouses of veterans. By giving them voice—indeed, the women on the receiving end of the violence perpetrated by the respondents documented in this book—perhaps a more sophisticated *intersectional* understanding will emerge. Indeed, confronting the experiences of female survivors will enable us to "better acknowledge and ground the differences among us and negotiate the means by which these differences will find expression."[7]

The stories of marginalized African-American male veterans, however, does provide a useful starting point. To put it as clearly as possible: *There is simply no legitimate reason for the kinds of cumulative suffering and traumatic experiences that befall African-American veterans and their families to occur in the first place.* The historical moment we find ourselves in calls for ideas that go right to the heart of the future of American democracy: It is a uniquely important opportunity in the history of the United States to think boldly about the future.[8] Fundamental to such an agenda is to acknowledge that America's war at home is inescapably about the meaning of citizenship in the lives of African-American veterans today. When citizenship is little more than *the right to survive* knowing where one's next meal will come from is by no means a guarantee.

"THE TRIPLE EVILS OF RACISM, ECONOMIC EXPLOITATION, AND MILITARISM"

Taken together the experiences of African-American veterans offer no easy solutions. Their collective plight is one that goes beyond tinkering with civilian or military bureaucracies. Instead, I believe it is far more productive to begin a larger dialogue with sociologist Joe R. Feagin's sobering acknowledgement that "our dominant social, economic, and political institutions do not yet imbed anything close to the old rhetorical ideal of 'liberty and justice for all,' or the related ideals of 'fairness and equality.'"[9]

Wealthy white political elites of recent eras continue to hastily plunge the nation into one destructive war after another. As the stories of the veterans in this book demonstrate, these actions have consequences that last for generations. Another major consequence of these wars has been to undermine the efforts of African-American civil rights activists who were tarred as "socialists" and "radicals." One fierce critic of the Vietnam War whose voice could not be silenced was Martin Luther King Jr.:

> Let me say finally that I oppose the war in Vietnam because I love America. I speak out against this war, not in anger, but with anxiety and sorrow in my heart, and, above all, with a passionate desire to see our beloved country stand as the moral example of the world. I speak out against this war because I am disappointed with America. And there can be no great disappointment where there is not great love. I am disappointed with our failure to deal positively and forthrightly with the triple evils of racism, economic exploitation, and militarism.[10]

In contrast to the empty white rhetorical ideals of "liberty and justice" and "fairness and equality," the longstanding legacies of the triple evils of racism, economic exploitation, and militarism brought to attention by black civil rights activists force us to go beyond vague criticisms of the Obama administration or the so-called military establishment. America's protracted emphasis on war has enabled white political and military elites to disengage with any real meaningful dialogue about the ongoing war at home and the countless racial and the human rights atrocities of countless racial and ethnic minorities slaughtered abroad.

The lies that led to the betrayal of African-American veterans—many who are now prisoners of America's ongoing racist wars on drugs and crime—implicate white elites from both ruling parties; failing the needs of veterans has been a longstanding bipartisan affair. Reflecting on the actions of white political and military elites goes a long way in teaching us about the longstanding betrayal of those veterans and non-veterans ravaged by the war at home. Even for those veterans, such as myself, that have benefitted from the GI Bill, the costly wars and the military-industrial complex that feeds them point to a bigger problem: the need for sweeping changes to the nation's educational and other opportunity programs. As does the desperate black veteran, who enlists because the military is the only steady work he can find. Such a longstanding state of affairs is a profound demonstration of the broader betrayal of the American worker. Veterans who only find health care after they have plunged into catastrophic illness are an indictment of America's entire health care system, as the stories of the uninsured so vividly illuminate. And on and on the cruel lessons of our wars go.

VETERANS HELPING OTHER VETERANS

> It started out of Milwaukee, Wisconsin, because black veterans who were returning from Vietnam were going to the vet center and would see a counselor and the counselor would turn on an egg timer and if you didn't explain your case before the egg timer stopped, they had you go to the back of the line and come back the next day. So they decided: "Hey we don't need that." So they started their own organization called the National Association of Black Veterans (NABVETS) and now there's like seventy groups throughout the country.
>
> —Lionel, Vietnam era veteran and former president of NABVETS-Baltimore

Although he continues to struggle financially, Lionel has remained active in the community. Most veterans I've interviewed were unfamiliar with NABVETS, and there has never been a Delaware chapter. What makes NABVETS remarkable is that it is not simply a black veteran's advocacy group, but an organization invested in the broader community. As Lionel described:

> We've adopted one of the poorest neighborhoods in Baltimore. We want to make a difference in the community. We come in with veterans who have knowledge, skills, and a building trade to literally start rebuilding. We're building a rec center as I speak and always doing extensive home repairs.

NABVETS-Baltimore is very cognizant of its supportive role and also tries to secure employment for black contractors in the area:

> We don't want to be perceived as some kind of occupying force. We are letting it be known to the community that you can count on us for help, but ultimately it will be you all that are the future. And we also go to meetings and fight for equal representation for black contractors. Because there's a big history of them being left out.

In addition to activism in the community and employment, Lionel describes NABVETS as aggressively inclusive:

> If you gonna rebuild then make sure that you have all minorities included, make sure you have veterans included, make sure that you have females included. . . . Make sure that you talk to the ladies to see where their kids need to be. . . . We make sure we talk to the seniors too; many of them need help getting to public transportation.

Lionel also informs me that NABVETS must continue to educate policy makers. Indeed, NABVETS aspiration to impact the day-to-day lives of people in Baltimore's impoverished communities serve as fitting last words to this book (See appendix for a list of veteran's advocacy organizations):

We have to educate the politicians and the bureaucrats as to what's available to them and through the federal government to assist the citizenry. We really want the organization to have some impact in the day-to-day lives of the people in these communities. But we know that the politicians love veterans as photo-op. We won't allow it! We're going to stay on them about the issues: compensation for PTSD, housing, disability. We're relentless and we won't stop. You know, just like the soldiers that we are [laughs].

Appendix

Veteran's Advocacy Organizations

BLACK VETERANS FOR SOCIAL JUSTICE INC.

www.bvsj.org

"Established in April 1979, Black Veterans for Social Justice Inc. (BVSJ) is a nonprofit, community-based organization in Brooklyn, New York, that has served men and women veterans, their families and members of the community for twenty-three years. BVSJ served an estimated 10,000 clients during 2002 with an annual budget of $10 million. Several programs aimed at helping homeless veterans operate under the direction of the organization, other services are provided through memorandums of understanding (MOUs) with local community-based organizations and government agencies."

—www.bvsj.org/

DISABLED AMERICAN VETERANS (DAV)

www.dav.org

"Disabled American Veterans has never wavered in our commitment to serve our nation's service-connected disabled veterans, their dependents and survivors. Our largest endeavor in fulfilling that mission is our National Service Program. In 88 offices throughout the United States and in Puerto Rico, the DAV employs a corps of approximately 260 National Service Officers (NSOs) who represent veterans and their families with claims for benefits from the Department of Veterans Affairs (VA), the Department of Defense and other government agencies. Veterans need not be DAV members to take advantage of this outstanding assistance, which is provided free of charge."

—www.dav.org/veterans/VeteransAffairs.aspx

IRAQ VETERANS AGAINST THE WAR

www.ivaw.org

The mission of IVAW is to mobilize the military community to withdraw its support for the wars and occupations in Iraq and Afghanistan. To achieve its mission, IVAW emphasizes three distinct goals: immediate withdrawal of all occupying forces in Iraq and Afghanistan; reparations for the human and structural damages suffered in Iraq and Afghanistan so that the peoples there might regain their right to self-determination; full benefits, adequate health-care (including mental health), and other supports for returning servicemen and women. Iraq Veterans Against the War has also passed resolutions opposing the war in Afghanistan, the Don't Ask, Don't Tell policy, and the occupation of Gaza, and in support of non-violence, immigrant rights, and the prosecution of the Bush administration for war crimes."

—www.ivaw.org/mission-and-goals

JAPANESE AMERICAN VETERANS ASSOCIATION (JAVA)

www.javadc.org/aboutus.htm

"JAVA is a fraternal, patriotic, educational, and historical organization with the purposes of preserving and strengthening comradeship among its members, perpetuating the memory and history of our departed comrades, maintaining true allegiance to the government of the United States of America, upholding its constitution and laws, and maintaining and extending the institutions of American freedom, and independently and in concert with other veterans organizations, striving to obtain for veterans, reservists, active duty military personnel and their families full benefit of their rightful entitlements as veterans."

—www.javadc.org/aboutus.htm

NATIONAL ASSOCIATION FOR BLACK VETERANS, INC. (NABVETS)

www.nabvets.org

"On an ongoing basis, the National Association for Black Veterans, Inc. will provide strategic advocacy on behalf of its membership with Congress, the federal administration, state administrations and other agencies and organizations. NABVETS will provide personal advocacy on behalf of veterans seeking claims against the United States Department of Veterans Affairs; advocacy for youth in all matters required for successful passage into adulthood; advocacy on behalf of families; with community involvement, provide advocacy in creating positive lifestyles for veterans; and to generate and preserve the historical record."

The NABVETS' mission statement can be found at www.nabvets.org/index.php/nabvets/about-nabvets/.

THE BUNKER PROJECT

http://bunkerproject4vets.org/

"The Bunker Project is not a treatment program and does not serve as a treatment facility but rather a practical, prevention-based support center that points the way to available treatment and resources available to veterans and their families. Provide 'reintegration bunkers' in strategic locations throughout the United States [that] provide a place where vets can feel safe, understood, and respected as they triage their situation and regroup and assess their needs when dealing with the culture-shock of reintegration. Provide 'mobile reintegration bunkers' for veterans who do not have access to established bunkers to meet and access as much of the resources as possible that are provided at established reintegration bunkers. This approach is especially valuable for providing veteran reintegration assistance for veterans who are in jail."

—http://bunkerproject4vets.org/

THE SOCIETY OF HISPANIC VETERANS

www.hispanicveterans.org

"The Society of Hispanic Veterans is a non-profit organization registered in the State of Florida. It was created to help and assist veterans in need, they offered us their lives, their arms and legs, their smiles. . . . It is now our time to offer them gratitude and respect. We are committed to honor and perpetuate the memory of deceased veterans and to assist their survivors; to assist hospitalized, disabled and needy war veterans and their dependents; to monitor and evaluate services delivered by government agencies and organizations to the veteran community, with the goal of ensuring that services are appropriate, relevant and of the highest quality; to educate, inform and assist members of the veteran community, their spouses and dependents in the areas of services and procedures, legal rights and responsibilities and issues of interest and concern to the veteran community; to be an information and referral source for veterans, their spouses and dependents in the areas of housing assistance, employment, job training, education, legal assistance, veterans benefits and government benefits."

—www.hispanicveterans.org/#!mission

VETERANS FOR PEACE

www.veteransforpeace.org

"Veterans For Peace is a national organization founded in 1985 by military veterans opposed to the Reagan administration's war against the people of Central America. It includes men and women veterans of all eras and duty stations spanning the Spanish Civil War, World War II, Korea, Vietnam, Panama, Persian Gulf, Bosnia, Afghanistan, Iraq, other conflicts and periods in between. Our collective experience tells us wars are easy to start and hard to stop and that those hurt are predominantly the innocent. We have over 100 chapters across the country, with a national office in Saint Louis, Missouri."

—www.veteransforpeace.org/who-we-are/our-mission/

VETERANS FOR COMMONSENSE

http://veteransforcommonsense.org

"Founded in 2002 by enlisted war veterans, Veterans for Common Sense (VCS) provides grass roots public policy advocacy, public relations, public education, and government relations. Based on the pragmatic ideals of the American patriot Thomas Paine, VCS works to raise the unique and powerful voices of veterans, so that our military, veterans receive a square deal. Veterans for Common Sense also strives to ensure that America's national security and long-term prosperity are protected and enhanced, for ourselves and for future generations. America can only live up to her highest ideals when all of her citizens are engaged in civil discourse. Veterans have risked their lives to defend the constitution and their country and have a vital role to play in this engagement. Veterans advocacy is nothing more than a continuation of service. Veterans for Common Sense is a nonprofit, 501(c)(3) charitable organization. We are supported primarily by individual donations from our members."

—http://veteransforcommonsense.org/about-vcs/

WOMEN VETERANS OF AMERICA

www.womenveteransofamerica.com

"Especially due to the current wars in Iraq and Afghanistan, it's difficult to go a day without considering the immense sacrifice of our military service members. But what happens to those service members after they are discharged and return to civilian life? The unique calling of military service means that our soldiers need support both on the ground and after they have come home. Women veterans face their own array of issues after they have finished active duty. We created WomenVeteransOfAmerica.com to be a resource for women veterans and for the families and friends who support them. On our site you can learn about women veterans' health issues, information on military sexual trauma, and the balancing of motherhood with service. We have also done our best to make veteran's benefits understandable and to direct readers toward useful organizations and resources advocating for women veterans. We are very grateful to all current and past members of the military service, and we wanted to make a helpful resource that reflects this."

—www.womenveteransofamerica.com/about

Notes

1. AFRICAN-AMERICAN VETERANS AND THE WAR AT HOME

1. To preserve confidentiality, all veterans' names appear as pseudonyms. Moreover, I sometimes changed details about experiences that I believed might compromise the respondent's confidentiality.

2. According to the American Psychiatric Association's latest *Diagnostic and Statistical Manual of Mental Disorders* (DSM-IV-TR), a PTSD diagnosis must include "a history of exposure to a traumatic event meeting two criteria and symptoms from each of three symptom clusters: intrusive recollections, avoidant/numbing symptoms, and hyper-arousal symptoms." http://www.ptsd.va.gov/professional/pages/dsm-iv-tr-ptsd.asp.

3. See Kai Erikson, *Everything in its Path: Destruction of Community in the Buffalo Creek Flood* (New York: Simon & Schuster, 1978), 153–154.

4. See Jeffrey Morenoff, Robert J. Sampson, and Stephen Raudenbush, 2001, "Neighborhood Inequality, Collective Efficacy, and the Spatial Dynamics of Urban Violence," *Criminology* 39, no. 3 (2001): 517–560.

5. For a classic sociological work that illuminates dynamic resilience and struggle in impoverished black kin networks, see Carol Stack, *All Our Kin: Strategies for Survival in a Black Community* (New York: Basic Books, 1974).

6. For a fascinating and sophisticated empirical account of impoverished blacks actively seeking employment, see Sandra Susan Smith, *Lone Pursuit: Distrust and Defensive Individualism Among the Black Poor* (New York: Russell Sage Foundation, 2007).

7. Wallace Terry's oral history provides perhaps the most viscerally powerful indictment of the systemic mistreatment experienced by black Vietnam era veterans. To understand the remarkable resolve of black veterans of the Korean War era, see Christopher S. Parker, *Fighting for Democracy: Black Veterans and the Struggle Against White Supremacy* (Princeton, NJ: Princeton University Press, 2009). For a comprehensive review of racial and gender inequity in the GI Bill, see Glenn S. Altschuler and Stuart M. Blumin, *The GI Bill: A New Deal for Veterans* (New York: Oxford University Press, 2009). Black veterans just back from World War I, experienced deplorable housing conditions and medial care (Mikkelsen, *Coming from Battle to Face a War* PhD diss., Florida State University, 2007, 98).

> Black soldiers also complained about unsanitary conditions on military bases. In Newport, Virginia, Charles H. Harris stated that he and his fellow black troops at Camp Stuart had to wash their mess kits in the same water as soldiers with venereal

diseases. Wounded veterans encountered obstacles when they sought medical treatment. Black citizens wrote to the NAACP demanding that the organization, as well as "Negro ministers," atone for the neglect of black soldiers. One outraged citizen described Walter Reed Hospital's treatment of black veterans: [O]ur Negro soldiers are cruelly and brutally treated . . . by a white nurse, who insolently refuses to prepare or order a prescribed diet for a Negro soldier who had his insides burn out by gas in France and otherwise afflicted [in] his country's battles. He was forced to lie all during the day of December 16th in Ward 35 without care, medicine, food or nourishment for no other reason than he is a Negro and proud of it. The soldier protested his inhuman treatment and asked the white patient to witness, when the white soldier in the ward threatened to come to his bed and club his brains out if he dared protest again.

8. See Gerald Nicosia, *Home to War, A History of the Vietnam Veterans Movement* (New York: Crown, 2001), 26.
9. See Myra MacPherson, *Long Time Passing: Vietnam and the Haunted Generation* (New York: Doubleday, 1984), 555–556.
10. See Nicosia, *Home to War*, 397.
11. See Bruce Western, *Punishment and Inequality* (New York: Sage, 2006), 91.
12. For one of several powerful critiques, see Thomas E. Ricks, *Fiasco: The American Military Adventure in Iraq* (New York: Penguin, 2006).
13. See Frances Fox Piven's remarkable book, *The War at Home: The Domestic Costs of Bush's Militarism* (New York: The New Press, 2004), 13.
14. See Wallace Terry, *Bloods: Black Veterans of the Vietnam War: An Oral History* (New York: Ballantine Books, 1984), xv.
15. For perhaps the most empirically sophisticated and enlightening studies of the political economy of black mass imprisonment, see Western, *Punishment and Inequality* (2006).
16. See Anne Leland and Mari-Jana "M-J" Oboroceanu, *American War and Military Operations Casualties: Lists and Statistics*, 2010). The report provides comprehensive statistics on military casualties from multiple eras and can be accessed online here: http://www.fas.org/sgp/crs/natsec/RL32492.pdf.
17. "The average unemployment rate for Blacks in 2011 was 15.8 percent compared to 7.9 percent for Whites." See U.S. Department of Labor, *The African-American Labor Force in the Recovery*, 2. The report can be accessed from the Department of Labor's website here: http://www.dol.gov/_sec/media/reports/BlackLaborForce/BlackLaborForce.pdf
18. "Among unemployed veterans in 2010, white veterans accounted for the bulk of the unemployed (78.1 percent), followed by Blacks or African-Americans (17.5 percent), *though they represent 11.9 percent of the veteran labor force* (emphasis added)." See U.S. Department of Labor, *The Veteran Labor Force in the Recovery*, 5. The report can be accessed from the Department of Labor's website here: http://www.dol.gov/_sec/media/reports/VeteransLaborForce/VeteransLaborForce.pdf.
19. While the history of racial oppression in America is anything but linear, I concur with Michelle Alexander that the mass incarceration of African-Americans and its subsequent mass impoverishing effects marks an unprecedented moment in history and is worthy of being called "The New Jim Crow." See Michelle Alexander, *The New Jim Crow: Mass Incarceration in the Age of Colorblindness* (New York: The New Press, 2010).
20. Some of the classics in this rich sociological tradition include, W.E.B. Du Bois, *The Philadelphia Negro: A Social Study* (Philadelphia: University of Pennsylvania Press, 1899); Ulf Hannerz, *Soulside: Inquiries into Ghetto Culture and Community* (Chicago: University of Chicago Press, 1969); Elliot Liebow, *Talley's Corner: A Study of Negro Street Corner Men* (Lanham, Maryland: Rowman & Littlefield,1967); Lee Rainwater, *Behind Ghetto Walls: Black Families in a Federal Slum* (Chicago: Aldine, 1970).
21. For a remarkable photographic display of the Wilmington race riots of 1968, see http://www.oldwilmington.net/oldwilmington/1968-riots.html.

22. All of the housing and demographic information reported here comes from a report by the Wilmington-based organization, *Housing for All,* that can be accessed online here: http://www.housingforall.org/rop0304%20full%20online.pdf

23. According to *Housing for All*, white flight in the city of Wilmington has increased exponentially in the post–civil rights era. Indeed, the city's white middle class population has remained on a steady decline since 1970. Cara Armbrister, "The Concentration of Poverty: Wilmington, Delaware." In: Housing for All (eds), *The Realities of Poverty in Delaware 2003–2004*. Wilmington, Delaware, 39-45. Available at: http://www.housingforall.org/rop0304%20full%20online.pdf (p. 140–141).

24. HOPE VI was established in 1996 by then HUD Secretary Henry Cisneros as a public housing demolition and redevelopment initiative established to "radically transform public housing in this country" by utilizing the "power of market discipline and individual choice." Henry Cisneros (1995) Written testimony, HUD reinvention: from blueprint to action. Hearing before the Subcommittee on Housing and Community Opportunity of the Committee on Banking and Financial Service, U.S. House of Representatives, 6 April. (page 71). Since 1998, HUD has awarded the city $16,820,350 in funding. In one of the clearest examples of how the city's use of HOPE VI funding has resulted in dramatic displacement of residents is the Village of Eastlake project. After the WHA demolished 267 units, the new development provided 160 units resulting in a shortfall of 107 units. See: http://www.whadelaware.org/hopevi.html.

25. See Adam Taylor, "The City's Approach to Policing," *The News Journal*, November 25, 2010, at http://www.sparkweekly.com/article/20101125/NEWS01/11250360.

26. The plan can be accessed online here: http://www.wilmingtonde.gov/redocuments/FY2011-2015-Consolidated-Plan-DRAFT072210.pdf.

27. See "FY2011-2015 Consolidated Plan," 91. City of Wilmington's Five-Year Strategic Plan (FYSP) 2011–2015, The plan can be accessed online at http://www.wilmingtonde.gov/redocuments/FY2011-2015-Consolidated-Plan-DRAFT072210.pdf. The overwhelming majority of my interviews with African-American veterans were conducted in Wilmington's most impoverished neighborhoods. These places are, in effect, exclusionary zones much like those seen in cities all across the United States, see Katherine Beckett and Steve Herbert, *Banished: The New Social Control in Urban America* (New York: Oxford University Press, 2009).

2. THE AFRICAN-AMERICAN VETERAN AS A SOCIAL PROBLEM

1. Current national strategies do little to create livable housing for veterans. Instead, programs such as the VA's recently established *National Call Center for Homeless Veterans* is largely reactive and focuses on emergency shelter and service to veterans who lack housing. For a description of the program, see: http://www.va.gov/health/NewsFeatures/20120220a.asp.

2. For an excellent empirical exploration of the impact of mass incarceration on impoverished communities of color, see Todd Clear *Imprisoning Communities: How Mass Incarceration Makes Disadvantaged Neighborhoods Worse* (New York: Oxford University Press, 2007).

3. Jason Adam Wasserman, Jeffrey Michael Clair, and Chelsea Platt "The "Homeless Problem" and the Double Consciousness," *Sociological Inquiry* (forthcoming).

4. In a focus group study of African-Americans experiences with white racism, researchers discovered how white hostility in the workplace profoundly drained respondents of the necessary energy to even relax during the weekends. See Joe R. Feagin and Karyn D. McKinney, *The Many Costs of Racism* (Lanham, Maryland: Rowman & Littlefield, 2002).

5. Mel's experience resonates deeply with the insights of W. E. B. Du Bois in his classic book, *The Souls of Black Folk* (New York: Bantam Books, 1903). Far more than a fatalistic vision, Du Bois's conception of black identity as a historically complex "double consciousness" is important for what it reveals about the possibilities of upward mobility and, indeed, the broader struggles in the lives of black veterans such as Mel and other veterans presented in the book.

6. See Michael Musheno and Susan Ross, *Deployed: How Reservists Bear the Burden of Iraq*, "Shadows of Vietnam," (Ann Arbor: University of Michigan Press, 2009), 15–24.

7. For a remarkable study using CIA documents and extensive archival research to show persuasively how Vietnam catalyzed the drug war at home, see Jeremy Kuzmaraov, *The Myth of the Addicted Army: Vietnam and the Modern War on Drugs* (Amherst: University of Massachusetts Press, 2009).

8. See Michelle Alexander, *The New Jim Crow: Mass Incarceration in the Age of Colorblindness* (New York: The New Press, 2010), 208.

9. See Michael Massing, *The Fix* (Berkeley: University of California Press, 2000),123.

10. See Lillian B. Rubin, *Busing and Backlash: White Against White in an Urban School District* (Berkeley: University of California Press, 1972), 208.

11. For an excellent study of the disturbingly punitive turn in school discipline in America's public schools, see Aaron Kupchik, *Homeroom Security: School Discipline in an Age of Fear* (New York: New York University Press, 2010).

12. See Jorge Mariscal, "Fighting the Poverty Draft" available online here: http://www.counterpunch.org/2005/01/28/fighting-the-poverty-draft/

13. See Paul Starr, *The Discarded Army: Veterans After Vietnam* (New York: David McKay Company, 1974), 167.

14. See Alford Young Jr., *The Minds of Marginalized Men: Making Sense of Mobility, Opportunity, and Future Life Chances* (Princeton, NJ: Princeton University Press, 2004), 26.

15. See Carol Stack, *All Our Kin: Strategies for Survival in a Black Community* (New York: Basic Books, 1974).

16. For a recent study documenting poor, African Americans as mentors and community activists, see Yasser Arafat Payne and Hanaa A. Hamdi "Street Love: How Street Life Oriented U.S. Born African Men Frame Giving Back to One Another and the Local Community," *The Urban Review* 41, n.1: 29–46.

17. Glenn S. Altschuler and Stuart M. Blumin, *The GI Bill: A New Deal for Veterans* (New York: Oxford University Press, 2009), 133.

18. Jeremy Kuzmarov, *The Myth of the Addicted Army: Vietnam and the Modern War on Drugs* (Amherst: University of Massachusetts Press, 2009).

19. My use of the term structural violence parallels medical anthropologist Paul Farmer's explanation: "[A]cts of violence are perpetrated, usually by the strong against the weak in complex social fields. . . . A set of historically given and, often enough, economically driven conditions—again termed "structural violence"—guarantee that violent acts will ensue." See Paul Farmer, *Pathologies of Power: Health, Human Rights, and the New War on the Poor* (Berkeley: University of California Press, 2005).

20. For an excellent intellectual biography of Johnson, see Patrick J. Gilpin and Marybeth Gasman, *Charles S. Johnson: Leadership Beyond the Veil of Jim Crow* (Albany, NY: State University of New York Press, 2003)

21. For a prescient account of political and economic marginality suffered by blacks in the post-bellum era, see W. E. B. Du Bois, *Black Reconstruction* (New York: Harcourt and Brace, 1935). After Reconstruction and deep into the twentieth century several other important sociohistorical and empirical accounts of persistent racial inequality have served to illuminate the stubborn persistence of black racial inequality in the United States. Stephen Grant documents the persistence of housing discrimination in all regions of the United States. Specifically, how a white supremacist groundswell combined with weakened federal legislation have perpetuated the continued legacy of racial segregation in housing. Meyer's book, moreover, illuminates a long history of white racism that sheds light on entrenched conditions of black marginalization in the contemporary United States more broadly. See Stephen Grant Meyer, *As Long as They Don't Move Next Door: Segregation and Racial Conflict in American Neighborhoods* (Lanham, Maryland: Rowman and Littlefield, 2000).

22. For an incisive critique of the current U.S Supreme Court, see Martin Garbus, *The Next 25 Years: The New Supreme Court* (New York: Seven Story Press, 2007). For a comprehensive analysis of the impact of systemic white racism on the lives of African Americans, see Joe R. Feagin, *Racist America: Roots, Current Realities, and Future Reparations* (2nd edition) (New York: Routledge, 2010).

23. In addition to Charles S. Johnson's seminal life experience studies on early twentieth-century racial inequality, Glenn H. Elder's study of 167 individuals born at the height of the Great Depression, provides a remarkable multi-generational study of economic crisis in the life course. See Glenn H. Elder, *Children of the Great Depression* (Boulder, CO: Westview Press, 1974). For a rich life history study of Americans with disabilities, see David M. Engel and Frank W. Munger, *Rights of Inclusion: Law and Disability in the Life Stories of Americans with Disabilities* (Chicago: University of Chicago Press, 2003).

24. See Young Jr., *The Minds of Marginalized Men*, 77–78.

3. JOINING UP

1. See Alair MacLean and Glen H. Elder, "Military Service in the Life Course," *Annual Review of Sociology 33* (2007): 188.

2. In addition to strictly enforcing income requirements that Lionel describes. "welfare offices continued to engage in midnight raids on the homes of ADC recipients in order to police 'man in the house' rules. The stated reason for surprise visits was to catch men sleeping in the homes of women receiving welfare. Unmarried women with men in their beds were deemed morally unfit and their households therefore unsuitable for assistance." See Kaaryn Gustafson, "The Criminalization of Poverty," *The Journal of Criminal Law and Criminology* 99, n.3 (2009), 649.

3. For an important documentation of the recent ascendancy of blacks in the ranks of the active duty army, see Charles C. Moskos and John Sibley Butler, *All that We Can Be: Black Leadership And Racial Integration The Army Way* (New York: Basic Books, 1996).

4. See Myra MacPherson, *Long Time Passing: Vietnam and the Haunted Generation* (New York: Doubleday, 1984).

5. Unfortunately due to increasing joint pain, Jeffrey was unable to elaborate and we mutually decided to end the interview early.

6. Given his subsequent emotional breakdown in the service (see chapter 4), it seems perhaps that the lack of counseling he received after his stepfather's suicide left lasting emotional scars that very well may have been connected to his own battles with mental illness he would fight years later.

4. IN THE SERVICE

1. See Myra MacPherson, *Long Time Passing: Vietnam and the Haunted Generation* (New York: Doubleday, 1984), 550–569.

2. See MacPherson, *Long Time Passing*, xi.

3. This useful concept for understanding the adaptation processes in the military experiences of black veterans is articulated by Joe R. Feagin as follows: "[B]lack Americans develop or enhance the important home-frames or counter-frames that help them to make sense out of the often difficult social worlds they find as they venture out of their communities into white-controlled institutional worlds." See Joe R. Feagin, *The White Racial Frame: Centuries of Racial Framing and Counter-Framing* (New York: Routledge, 2010), 180.

4. The "cool pose" in Terrence's experience is, although ultimately characterized by a loss of control of surroundings, closest to what Majors and Billson describe as "cool as the ultimate control":

> For many black males cool pose is a way to say, "you might break my back but not my spirit." Cool pose is the black man's last-ditch effort for masculine self-control . . .The young black male sees control in terms of having a weak or strong

> mind. If he loses control, he becomes dangerously vulnerable to pressures that he fears will undermine him or "blow his mind." Cool helps him get and stay in control over his psychological and social space.

See Richard Majors and Janet Mancini Billson, *Cool Pose: The Dilemmas of Black Manhood in America* (New York: Touchstone, 1993), 29.

5. THE JOURNEY HOME

1. Lembcke insightfully shows how "the bad Vietnam veteran" was a pervasive way post-war media coverage was able to deny the profoundly traumatizing effects experienced by those who bravely served, including respondents like Carl whose combat experiences resulted in numerous stays in VA psychiatric wards. The association between mental illness and Vietnam veterans was deepened in the text of the story, which was peppered with such phrases as "serious readjustment problems," "emotional stability," "shattering stability," "psychiatric casualty," "mental health disaster," "social problem," "emotionally disturbed," "men with damaged brains," and "severe depression." Even its attempts to appear discriminating in its characterizations, the story managed to cast a pall over veterans: "The men who suffer post-Vietnam syndrome are not dramatically ill. They do not go berserk or totally withdraw. Instead, they are bewildered, disillusioned, unable to cope."
See Jerry Lembcke, *The Spitting Image: Myth, Memory, and the Legacy of Vietnam* (New York: New York University Press, 1998), 103.

2. Perhaps the most empirically rigorous critique of "Broken Windows Theory," the leading rationale for so called "quality of life" policing. See Robert J. Sampson and Stephen W. Raudenbush, "Systematic Social Observation of Public Spaces: A New Look at Disorder in Urban Neighborhoods," *American Journal of Sociology* 105, n. 3 (1999): 603–651.

6. "WE THANK YOU FOR YOUR SERVICE"

1. Of course, this sentiment is not meant to downplay the efforts of organizations such as the National Association for Black Veterans (NABVETS).

2. See Gerald Nicosia, *Home to War: A History of the Vietnam Veterans Movement* (New York: Crown, 2001), 618.

3. One of the disturbing revelations of this hearing was that the VA has no coordinated outreach effort to reach impoverished African-American veterans, see African-American Veterans and Community: Post-Traumatic Stress Disorder and Related Issues: Hearing Before the Subcommittee on Oversight and Investigations, of the House Committee on Veterans' Affairs, 103rd Cong. 5 (1993) (Questioning of VA representatives by Rep. Maxine Waters).

4. For a scathing organizational and political critique of the VA in AVF Era, see Martin Schram, Vets Under Siege: *How America Deceives and Dishonors Those Who Fight Our Battles* (New York: St. Martin's Press, 2008).

5. See Kai Erikson, *Everything in its Path: Destruction of Community in the Buffalo Creek Flood* (New York: Simon & Schuster, 1978), 153–154.

6. See Sherman, Michelle D, Fred Sautter, M. Hope Jackson, Judy A. Lyons, Xiaotong Han, "Domestic Violence in Veterans with Post-Traumatic Stress Disorder Who Seek Couples Therapy," *Journal of Marital and Family Therapy* (2007), n. 4: 479–490.

7. Kimberlé Crenshaw, "Mapping the Margins: Intersectionality, Identity Politics, and Violence Against Women of Color," *Stanford Law Review* 43, 1298.

8. Sociologist Joe R. Feagin presents an ambitious and thought provoking antiracist agenda in his book *Racist America*. Feagin argues that only sweeping changes in U.S. education, law (e.g., a new U.S. constitution and reparations), and a more expansive view of antiracist efforts as both intersectional and global in reach will suffice. Moreover, Feagin's call for a more aggressive adoption of the Universal Declaration of Human Rights (UDHR) by judges and state elites is especially critical in light of America's insatiable appetite for imperialism and its erroneously conceived wars. While the United States has yet to sign onto any of the UDHR's conventions, embracing global peace efforts is essential for improving conditions both abroad and on the home front.

9. See Joe R. Feagin, *The White Racial Frame: Centuries of Racial Framing and Counter-Framing* (New York: Routledge, 2010), 193.

10. Martin Luther King Jr.: "Why I Am Opposed to the War in Vietnam," Sermon at the Ebenezer Baptist Church on April 30, 1967, available online at http://husseini.org/2007/01/martin-luther-king-jr-why-i-am.html.

Index

About the Author

Benjamin Fleury-Steiner is associate professor of sociology and criminal justice at the University of Delaware. He is coeditor of *The New Civil Rights Research*, a Choice Outstanding Academic Title. He is a veteran of Operation Desert Storm and was an enlisted military police officer in the U.S. Army from 1990 to 1993.